"What a joy to read *The Art and Skill of Buddhist Meditation*. This book is filled with the author's warmth, wisdom, and compassion. Richard Shankman has offered a very clear and user-friendly companion for anyone wanting to learn meditation.... A great gift."

—**Bob Stahl, PhD**, coauthor of *A Mindfulness-Based Stress Reduction Workbook, Living with Your Heart Wide Open, Calming the Rush of Panic, A Mindfulness-Based Stress Reduction Workbook for Anxiety*, and *MBSR Every Day*

"A wonderfully clear, simple yet thorough book on how to practice Buddhist meditation! Richard Shankman does a masterful job at guiding us through the natural and powerful interplay of mindfulness, concentration, and insight. Whether you are new to meditation or an experienced practitioner, this is a book to keep close at hand."

—**Tara Brach, PhD**, author of *Radical Acceptance* and *True Refuge*

"In simple, clear language, [Shankman] shares how mindfulness, concentration, and insight form one complete path. A wonderful guide for practice! While valuable for anyone, people who can't easily access a meditation teacher or supportive community will especially appreciate this book."

—**Sharon Salzberg**, author of *Lovingkindness* and *Real Happiness*

"A brilliant introduction to meditation practice. Infused with Richard Shankman's compassion, this practical and wise book provides the tools needed for individuals to deepen their practice and find their own way on the path of meditation."

—**Gil Fronsdal**, teacher at Spirit Rock Meditation Center and Insight Meditation Center, and author of *The Issue at Hand, A Monastery Within*, and a translation of *The Dhammapada*

"Richard Shankman's new book, *The Art and Skill of Buddhist Meditation*, is a wonderfully clear and straightforward guide for deepening our understanding of the meditative process. Based on his many years of practice and study, he offers a unified vision of the path, with many helpful and practical suggestions all along the way. An important contribution for navigating the inner journey."

—**Joseph Goldstein**, author of *Mindfulness*

"Here is a book that you will turn to again and again over the years of your practice because it speaks to both the possibilities and the challenges of meditation. Richard Shankman offers clear instructions on how to establish a meditation practice as well as specific guidance through some of the deepest practices of concentration and insight."

—**Phillip Moffitt**, author of *Dancing with Life* and *Emotional Chaos to Clarity*

"This book is like having a skilled meditation coach by your side. Richard will teach you the basics of meditation, and then keep refining your approach, anticipating the highs and lows you'll meet over years of practice. He combines ease of understanding with a real depth in both concentration and insight. This book offers valuable tips for both new and experienced meditators."

—**Guy Armstrong**, senior teacher at Spirit Rock Meditation Center and the Insight Meditation Society

THE
ART AND SKILL
OF BUDDHIST
MEDITATION

mindfulness, concentration, and insight

RICHARD SHANKMAN

New Harbinger Publications, Inc.

Publisher's Note

This publication is designed to provide accurate and authoritative information in regard to the subject matter covered. It is sold with the understanding that the publisher is not engaged in rendering psychological, financial, legal, or other professional services. If expert assistance or counseling is needed, the services of a competent professional should be sought.

Distributed in Canada by Raincoast Books

Translations in Chapter 8 of the jhana definitions are by the author.

Translations of the jhana similes are reprinted with permission:
Excerpts from *The Middle Length Discourses of The Buddha: A New Translation of the Majjhima Nikâya*, translated by Bhikkhu Ñânamoli, edited and revised by Bhikkhu Bodhi. Copyright © 1995 by Bhikkhu Bodhi. Reprinted with the permission of The Permissions Company, Inc., on behalf of Wisdom Publications, http://www.wisdompubs.org.

Cover design by Amy Shoup; Interior design by Michele Waters-Kermes; Acquired by Jess O'Brien; Edited by Ken Knabb

Library of Congress Cataloging-in-Publication Data

Shankman, Richard.
  The art and skill of Buddhist meditation : mindfulness, concentration, and insight / Richard Shankman.
    pages cm
  ISBN 978-1-62625-293-6 (paperback) -- ISBN 978-1-62625-294-3 (pdf e-book) -- ISBN 978-1-62625-295-0 (epub) 1. Meditation--Buddhism. 2. Theravada Buddhism. I. Title.
  BQ5612.S525 2015
  294.3'4435--dc23
                          2015014898

MIX
Paper from responsible sources
FSC® C011935
www.fsc.org

Printed in the United States of America

17   16   15

10   9   8   7   6   5   4   3   2   1   First printing

CONTENTS

INTRODUCTION

Perhaps nothing is more emblematic of Buddhism than the image of a monk in silent meditation. With closed eyes and attention inward drawn, it evokes in us a sense of wisdom, peace, and calm.

Ever since the Buddha's great awakening and discovery of a long-forgotten path to inner peace and happiness, meditators have followed in his footsteps. Ordinary people just like us have undertaken the same practices that have been handed down throughout the centuries. They have seen for themselves the treasures these teachings might hold in their own lives. We can realize the peace and happiness the Buddha discovered 2500 years ago.

This book is a travel guide along that same path to inner peace, meditation as it has been preserved and taught in the Theravada tradition of Buddhism. Theravada means "school of the elders" and is the oldest living Buddhist tradition, the only one of the earliest Buddhist schools surviving today. Its texts are preserved in the Pali language.

This is a book of exploration and discovery. We will explore the essential elements of meditation, from beginning mindfulness to the deeper stages of concentration and insight—learning how to cultivate and strengthen them, and how to bring them together in our practice. We will discover the greatness of our capacity for wisdom, love, and kindness as we open to deep states of calm, clarity, and peace.

Meditation is not something mysterious or complicated. Meditation is accessible and practical. Its benefits are available for anyone interested in discovering what it may have to offer. Its practices and techniques are simple to do. Meditation is about learning how to live peacefully with quiet minds and open hearts. All the things we may have heard about that can come from meditation— wisdom, peace, and calm—we can realize for ourselves.

Buddhist meditation comprises a variety of practices for calming our mind and increasing awareness of our thoughts, moods, and emotions. Being more aware of our experience offers the chance for meeting any situation in a more balanced way. We have the possibility to respond wisely when we can be more fully present and less reactive with whatever happens. We learn to move through all the ups and downs of life with balance and an inner sense of well-being.

Why Meditate?

You may be drawn to meditation for many reasons. You may be looking for a way to manage your stress and feel more peaceful and calm. Perhaps you want to quiet your mind, which is scattered all over the place, to stop obsessing and learn to relax. Or you are dealing with chronic pain or illness, or any other challenging situation that is hard to endure, and you are looking for tools to help. Sometimes we don't know exactly what we are looking for, but we know we are suffering or struggling in some way and have heard that meditation might help.

All of these benefits are available to us. Peace and joy may seem distant, but they are in actuality not so far away. They are within each of us, but we must turn our attention inward and come to know ourselves. With practice your mind will become trained and a natural sense of calm and contentment will follow.

The ultimate goal of Buddhist meditation and teachings is to guide us toward a nonreactive equanimity and inner peace in the midst of all aspects of our lives. Beyond the importance and benefit of fostering the valuable skills of stress reduction, pain management, and relaxation, on a more fundamental level Buddhist teachings are asking us to make a shift in how and where we look for happiness, with far-reaching and profound consequences for our well-being.

Buddhist meditation is a mosaic of wise and skillful means for cultivating wholesome qualities of our hearts and minds, enabling us to live and act in ways that create more happiness and less suffering for others and ourselves. We can learn to respond skillfully to any situation, with wisdom rather than reactivity. As we move about our daily lives with increasing open-heartedness and calm, we can meet our difficulties and learn to work with them.

The Buddha's Teaching

Buddhism is a down-to-earth, practical teaching. It is not interested in metaphysics or philosophy but, rather, in concrete steps we can apply directly to our life. The Buddha was inviting us to take an honest look at our life situation and ourselves. He was helping us find a way to lasting peace and happiness in the midst of life *as it is*.

The Buddha's teachings, known as *dharma*, offer a framework for understanding our world and ourselves. Though these teachings can seem complicated or imposing, their essence is expressed in a concise, yet comprehensive, formula: the Four Noble Truths.

The First Noble Truth is that life involves suffering, that life contains an unavoidable element of uncertainty and stress. One of the most misunderstood of all Buddhist concepts is the teaching on suffering. Many people believe the Buddha taught that life *is* suffering, but this a misconception. Buddhism acknowledges the obvious fact that life contains both happiness and misery, pleasure and pain.

It is not that there is no happiness to be found in this life. Getting happiness by having more of what we want and getting rid of experiences we do not like certainly bring their own rewards. But those rewards are not enduring. No experience will give us a stable, secure sense of satisfaction because everything is constantly changing and nothing is going to last.

Seeking our happiness solely in having or not having certain experiences—we call that a *conditioned happiness*, because it is dependent on circumstances—is a fragile kind of well-being. Even when things are going well, we know that the security and happiness of the moment will ultimately be lost. On some level we know that life is uncertain, tenuous at best, and that anything can happen at any time. This can leave us feeling uneasy, never really at peace. Because everything is destined to change, we suffer when we cling to anything, when we try to hold on to what cannot last or fight against our experience when it is not to our liking.

This is the First Noble Truth, that life is uncertain and unreliable. We can appreciate the happiness of the moment, but when the situation inevitably changes we suffer if we try to hold on to the past we long for or push away the present we wish to be different than it is. We do not suffer if we can learn to let go and be at peace with the ever-changing flow of life.

The Second Noble Truth is that the suffering in our lives has a cause. This cause is usually translated as desire or craving. Another common misconception is that Buddhism teaches that desire is bad, that we are supposed to get rid of all desires. But the Buddha stressed the importance of wholesome desire. If you did not desire to understand Buddhist teachings and apply them in your life, you would not be drawn to meditation.

Most of us spend most of our time striving to get or hold on to more of those situations, people, and things we think will make us happy, and avoiding those we think will make us unhappy. We seek to have more pleasant experiences and fewer unpleasant ones. No one wants to have less of what they want and more of what they don't want in life. When things are not going our way, we can't wait for them to change. And when things are going well, we forget, we become complacent and caught up in our daily affairs, thinking everything will just continue on and on as it has been. But sometimes you get what you want and sometimes you do not, and sometimes you get what you do not want at all.

So the Second Noble Truth is that we create suffering by clinging to things or pushing them away, all because of a particular kind of desire: craving. Through wholesome desire we are motivated and inspired to seek what is beneficial and good for ourselves and others. When healthy desire turns into craving, we cannot stand to be without those things or to let them go. When we are craving, our desire is so strong that we must have it, keep it, or get rid of it.

The Third Noble Truth is that there is an end to suffering. The enlightenment the Buddha discovered is often called a liberation through nonclinging. We can learn to ride the waves, navigating life's inevitable ups and downs with balance and grace. We can learn to let go of our suffering and live peacefully with quiet minds and open hearts in the midst of all that life gives us. All Buddhist teachings, and all the various meditation practices and techniques, are aids in service of this goal.

In the Fourth Noble Truth, the Buddha laid out a system for how to live and practice in order to cultivate wholesome qualities of our hearts and minds. This system is the Noble Eightfold Path. The first two elements of the Eightfold Path, Right Understanding (also known as Right View) and Right Intention, make up the wisdom section, and entail understanding the Buddha's teachings in order to aim one's efforts in the right direction. The morality or virtue section comprises the next three pieces, Right Speech, Right Action, and Right Livelihood. The final section is the path of meditation, the focus of this book, consisting of Right Effort, Right Mindfulness, and Right Concentration.

The Eightfold Path is a holistic system. Each factor is necessary for and dependent upon all the others. Most of this book focuses on the meditation section of the Eightfold Path but you cannot bypass the other elements, and they will be incorporated throughout the discussions. Without the wisdom to understand where you are aiming you cannot reach your goal, so you need Right Understanding and Right Intention. And your mind cannot settle down in meditation if you are mistreating others or embroiled in conflict, so you need to establish a foundation of virtue: Right Speech, Right Action, and Right Livelihood.

The Building Blocks of Meditation

Meditation aims us toward a more reliable way to find happiness, in which our well-being is not left to chance and life's uncertainties. Meditation is learning to let go of our obsessive tendencies of grasping for things we want and pushing away those we do not like, and to begin to look for happiness in how we relate to what is happening. We can find peace in any circumstance by letting go of craving and clinging, and by changing how we relate to whatever life brings us.

The concept of letting go and nonclinging is simple, but we soon find out that what sounds so simple, letting go of our suffering, is hard to do. To actualize this, we need to train our minds to more thoroughly learn how to let go. Our reactive patterns are strong and it is so easy for us to get caught over and over in our daily lives. If we say, "Do not cling to things or push anything away," perhaps we can do it in a given moment, but as soon as the right experience finds us, the particular causes and conditions arise—we are caught once again in our habitual reactive patterns. This is the place for meditation.

There are many meditation practices and they all aim to develop the key qualities of loving-kindness, compassion, mindfulness, concentration, and insight.

Loving-Kindness and Compassion

A balanced meditation practice, as well as a balanced life, is built upon a foundation of kindness and compassion. Some people find their hearts opening naturally as mindfulness, concentration, and insight grow. For others it is helpful to devote part or all of their practice to developing such kindness and compassion.

Compassion for ourselves supports us in difficult times, when we are struggling to find a way to let go. Compassion for others helps us relate to them with empathy and kindness, instead of reactivity and aversion. We learn how to engender kind thoughts and feelings and how to work skillfully to let go of negativity, seeking to suffuse a compassionate attitude into our meditation and our lives.

Mindfulness

Meditation begins with mindfulness. I define mindfulness in a simple way, as not being lost on "automatic pilot." Mindfulness means knowing whatever is happening rather than being caught up in your experience. It means being aware of yourself and your surroundings, not just going through the motions unaware of what you are doing. Being mindful means being awake to and fully present in any moment.

You can be mindful of anything. You can be aware of your thoughts and moods, what is happening in your body and what is going on around you. When you know your emotions without being entangled in them, you are able to make wise choices in how to respond to situations. You gain a balanced perspective that allows for greater freedom in meeting the flow of life's ups and downs.

Becoming more aware of your own experience, of what is happening in your mind and body, also helps foster a greater understanding of what *other* people are going through. You can notice those around you and how you are interacting with them. Having some space between your experience and your response to it opens you to greater possibilities and choice in how to act. Recognizing your mental and emotional patterns, you can begin to shift habitual behaviors.

In this book we will explore various ways to use and direct your attention in a purposeful way to strengthen concentration and insight. The first meditation practice I will offer is called mindfulness of breathing. This practice will help you learn how to connect with your breathing, so that your mind will grow more steady, more calm, and less distracted.

Concentration

Through the proper use of mindful attention you will learn how to compose and settle your mind, developing the quality of concentration. To be concentrated means your awareness is calm, collected, and undistracted. To be undistracted means your mind is not constantly wandering. You can direct your focus where and when you want and keep it there. A concentrated mind is amazingly clear and perceptive, beyond what is normally accessible.

With a steady, undistracted awareness, mindfulness can penetrate deeply and subtly as you turn your attention inward. A concentrated mind is described as being rid of impurities, bright, free from blemishes, flawless, pliable, adaptable, steady, and composed and collected. It is with this quality of mind that we turn toward insight.

Insight

We do not need the Buddha to tell us about suffering and stress. We know all about it. What we do not know, and what we need help with, is what to do about it. This is where insights can really help us.

A lot of emphasis is put on insight in Buddhist meditation. Insight means understanding the way things are, including life's uncertain and impermanent nature, and acknowledging and making peace with life on its own terms. We come to understand the inner workings of our mind and the nature of our body as it ages.

Insight blossoms as we connect with and come to know ourselves deeply and intimately. Increasingly, as mindfulness and concentration grow, we are able to clearly and directly perceive ever-subtler places of reactivity, their causes, and the way to let them go. We can see our habitual patterns and tendencies that lead to stress. We know when we are caught in those patterns and tendencies and understand how to let go of stress through nonclinging.

In the Buddha's path of awakening we seek to strengthen mindfulness and steady our minds in order to more clearly see things the way they really are. How to do this is the subject of this book.

Paths of Meditation

The various meditation practices all belong to one of three main branches of the meditation family: insight meditation, concentration meditation, and concentration and insight integrated as a single style of practice. Concentration and insight are both important in all these meditative paths. Because there is not just one way meditation is practiced and taught, there can be some confusion about how these two aspects of the practice fit together.

Insight meditation is often viewed and taught as a practice separate and distinct from concentration meditation. In this understanding, insight is equated with mindfulness, the present-moment awareness of whatever is happening. In the path of insight meditation—*vipassana* in Pali (pronounced vih-PAH-suh-nuh)—you apply mindfulness to meet your moment-to-moment experience, without any special effort devoted to cultivating concentration. Some degree of concentration will develop naturally as you sustain your attention on the array of experiences coming and going during the meditation session.

By paying attention to what is happening in each moment, you begin to clearly perceive and have insight into where you are clinging to or fighting against your experience. You start to learn how to meet difficulties and work with your suffering wisely. Meditators practicing in this style may not be concerned with developing the deeper stages of concentration, feeling that however much concentration naturally develops through mindful attention to their changing experiences is sufficient.

In the path of concentration meditation, you are concerned with the attainment of meditative states of highly undistracted awareness. Concentration meditation primarily seeks to calm and steady the mind. Some degree of insight develops naturally, as a result of being so undistracted, but the emphasis is on attaining deep stages of concentration known as *jhana*. (We will explore jhana in depth in a later chapter.) Those meditating in this way feel that refining their ability to remain undistracted enhances insight, and so they may turn to the practices of insight meditation only after developing concentration to a high degree.

In this book we are going to explore the third branch of meditation, in which concentration and insight are brought together as a single path of practice. In this style of meditation, concentration and insight are given equal emphasis. The aim is to develop the deeper levels of each, keeping both in mind at every step.

How to Use This Book

The practice presented here synthesizes mindfulness, concentration, and insight into a single, integrated path of meditation practice. I will offer specific guidance for cultivating both insight and concentration. This book will help you find the approaches and techniques that work best for you, offering a range of instructions for working with various possibilities of what can happen in meditation. Although no book can address every possible experience you can have in meditation, I will discuss the most common experiences that tend to arise as the meditation process unfolds, as well as a range of techniques suitable for dealing with those experiences.

Your task will be to engage in the various practices as best you can, and see what results you get. What you do next will depend on your experience from the previous practice. We do not want to bounce around from one thing to another, but we do want to remain receptive to see if something really is not working and to be ready to let it go and try something else.

This book is designed for both beginning and experienced meditators. Even if you are experienced, I suggest reading the first couple of chapters to get a sense of how concentration and insight can come together as one path.

If you are new to meditation, see what practices you are drawn to. Some will resonate with you. Give them a try. Some you will not relate to at all. Let those go. If you do not know or have a sense of which practice to use, pick mindfulness of breathing and stay with that a while. With time and with experience you will come to know what works and what does not. In subsequent chapters I will talk about how to proceed, depending on what happens as your meditation practice develops.

You should not expect to be an expert meditator in a single day. When learning anything new, it can take patience and perseverance to see results. Do not be surprised, and do not be hard on yourself, if you find it is not easy to sit quietly with yourself. Through repetition, and some degree of trial and error, we go from those clumsy first steps to a sense of proficiency and ease.

I am often asked how much time you should devote to meditation. The answer is however much you are inclined to do and your life circumstances will allow. Many people find that beginning with fifteen to twenty minutes a day is a good way to start. Once you have gained some experience, try sitting a little longer, perhaps half an hour. See how that works for you. Some people work their way up to forty-five minutes or an hour, or more, or sit more than once a day. In general, as with anything you wish to develop, the more time you give to meditation, the more you will get out of it. Just do the best you can. Any amount of time spent sitting quietly will be of benefit.

As you begin, take some time to reflect on your aspirations and intentions for undertaking these ancient practices. You would not be drawn to meditation and Buddhist teachings if you did not want to live with more clarity, calmness, wisdom, and compassion, in a way that creates less suffering and more well-being for yourself and others.

Keeping your good intentions in mind will be a great support through all the ups and downs of a meditative life as you begin this journey of awakening, following in the Buddha's footsteps.

Chapter 1

ESTABLISHING THE FOUNDATION FOR MEDITATION

Meditation comprises a wide array of skillful means. There are many meditation practices to choose from. Even if we all undertook the same meditation practice, regardless of what that practice entailed, we would have our own individual experiences.

Though we have many things in common, we are also unique and meditation unfolds differently for each of us. As a result, how best to work and what is needed in order to proceed at each step will be different for each of us. There is no single right or best technique or approach that is suitable for everyone, and so no instruction will be appropriate for all of us in all circumstances, no method universally effective or desirable in all situations. What is most useful for one person in dealing with a particular situation or experience may not prove useful for the next person, and may actually be counterproductive.

Concentration and insight, and all the various meditation practices and techniques for developing them, rest upon the foundation of mindfulness. Mindfulness means being aware of whatever is happening in any given moment. When you are angry or worried or stressed, you know it. When you are happy and at ease, you know that. You know your internal world, the feelings in your body, your emotions, thoughts, and moods, and you are mindful of the world around you. Whatever is happening, you can be mindful of it. In the next chapter you will learn specific practices to begin applying mindfulness in meditation, starting with mindfulness of breathing.

Through the practice of mindfulness you train your mind to settle and focus by directing your attention purposefully in a skillful way, and your ability to remain collected and stable increases. Being undistracted means your awareness can remain steady, without jumping around or wandering away. We use that undistracted awareness to more clearly come to know whatever is happening moment by moment, leading to insight. Practicing mindfulness leads to insight because you are looking directly into the nature of your own mind, body, and all experience.

Concentration and insight work together. Each can be a doorway for opening to the other. We must enlist them both, though one or the other may be emphasized at any particular time.

If you begin with concentration, you have to employ all the resources and support of mindfulness. You are making your mind steady, collected, and undistracted, so that your attention is not scattered. Your perceptions become powerful and the deepening of insight must follow.

If you emphasize insight in your meditation, you use mindfulness to investigate the conditioned and changing nature of your mind, your body, and all phenomena. You cannot help but strengthen and bring to bear the power of a steady mind. You may naturally incline in one direction or the other, but concentration and insight can never really be separated.

The more concentrated you are, the clearer and more refined your mind becomes and, because your awareness is unclouded, insights come on profound levels. A clear steady awareness illuminates your mind, allowing previously inaccessible and subtle areas of clinging and suffering to be revealed, so that you can see whether or not you truly are resting peacefully in the stream of nonclinging. Your perceptions are not only more subtle; because of concentration's penetrative power, their ability to permeate and transform you is greatly enhanced.

Sometimes you may choose to lean more on the concentration side and other times you might emphasize the deepening of insight. And sometimes meditation will take you in a direction other than what you intended. The emphasis in another direction will emerge on its own. We want to remain receptive to how our experience changes over the course of days or weeks, or throughout a single meditation session, and to be open to letting go of how we think things are supposed to be.

As your practice develops, the times when concentration is strong—when the mind is settled, clear, and sharp and it is easy to let other experiences stay in the background—will increase. During those times, remain simply with mindfulness of your breathing, or with other practices I will offer, working skillfully to strengthen the concentration, letting it run as far and deep as it can go. You will have lots of opportunities for insight to develop within the concentration practice since, through the deepening clarity concentration brings, you will naturally become more and more aware of a full range of experiences in your body and states of your mind and heart.

There will also be many times when you will not be able to concentrate. Your mind may become dull or scattered, or you may have to deal with hindrances or suffering in some way. Something you do not like will push to the forefront of your awareness and you will find yourself struggling or tense. You will naturally find yourself on the insight side of practice as you learn how to work in these situations. All of these times, when you cannot concentrate, when difficulties arise, as well as the times throughout your day outside of meditation, are rich areas for insight to grow as you learn to meet them with a quiet mind and open heart.

Even when your concentration is strong and your mind is clear and bright, you may choose to turn your attention toward investigating your experience, whether it is bringing mindfulness to meet some thought, emotion, or sensation in the body, or specifically looking for the characteristics of any experience, such as how it arises and passes away. In those times you are choosing to turn toward the insight side of the practice. You do not have to try and figure out when those times are, but can just follow your intuition where it leads you.

Dharma practice entails working skillfully with whatever is before you, with what is happening right now, right here in your experience. By remaining attuned to the natural unfolding of meditation, your experience will tell you what is needed, and whether you are on the concentration side of the practice or when the emphasis turns to insight.

What Does a Healthy Meditation Practice Look Like?

Before starting any practice or technique, we must establish a base of Right Understanding and Right Intention and have a basic idea of what our goals are. Bringing a sense of ease to your practice will help you relax into the present moment without overstriving, allowing you to meet and work skillfully with all that can happen in meditation. If you can meet your experience with an attitude of kindness and self-compassion, you will avoid falling into self-criticism or struggle during the times of challenge. Patience prepares you for working with any hindrances that may arise. These are the foundations upon which meditation is built.

Balanced Effort

In this practice we are trying both to get somewhere and to go nowhere at all, doing two apparently contradictory things at the same time. Sometimes dharma practice is talked about in terms of "going nowhere" or "nothing to gain," so it can seem confusing when we speak of cultivating or attaining meditative states of concentration and insight. These two aspects of practice, progressing along a path and going nowhere, appear to be at odds.

You would not undertake anything if you did not want to get something from it. Of course we want to be more concentrated, more peaceful, more quiet and clear. It's okay to want that—in fact the Buddha said that the pleasure of concentration should be pursued, developed, and cultivated.

This seeming contradiction resolves itself when we understand that we are actually doing only one thing: aiming ourselves in a wholesome direction and, at the same time—at each step along the path—resting aware of and present with whatever is happening. We are moving along a path of practice by cultivating and strengthening meditative states and wholesome qualities of our mind and heart, and we do it simply by staying present with and connecting mindfully with whatever is happening, moment by moment. Getting somewhere and going nowhere are both true at the same time.

The deeper stages of concentration are not stages of gaining or doing, but profound states of letting go. How can we want something while letting go of desire for it to happen? How can we devote ourselves to a path of progress, pursue it wholeheartedly, without making it an object of craving and clinging?

Our task is to learn how to get it but not grasp for it. As your mind begins to steady and the momentum of concentration builds, you learn to apply yourself ever more skillfully, recognizing more clearly what works and what is not helpful. By remaining mindful and clearly aware, not only of what is happening but how you are relating to what is happening, mental steadiness and clarity deepen and you can stay connected with equanimity and ease. Practicing in this way, our goals for developing wholesome qualities of calm, clarity, and peace do not become corrupted into overstriving. We want to apply ourselves well, but not fall away from a peaceful abiding in the present moment into longing for something else.

Right Effort is nonstriving effort. The idea of effort often connotes a sense of hard work and a determined push. I am suggesting another approach, a balanced effort that is skillful and that has nothing to do with striving or straining and everything to do with ease and relaxation, with maintaining a sense of connecting and allowing within mindful presence.

If we think there is something we have to attain, some place we have to reach, or any experience we must get other than the one we are having, we are out of balance; but we are also out of balance and do ourselves a disservice if we become complacent. Knowing when to make effort and when to relax and just allow is an art—an art that can take time and experience to cultivate and that comes for most people through a certain degree of trial and error. Try to let go of any expectation, resting as relaxed as you can in your present-moment experience, and then to practice in a way that naturally leads to deepening.

Ups and downs in energy, enthusiasm, and interest all come and go. At times you may notice a real decrease in wanting to meditate. Sometimes you will be motivated and sometimes you may be bored, even with pleasant meditative states. We can experience inspiring states of meditation and then feel bogged down in aversion or resistance.

When you hit a wall, sometimes the best thing to do is to keep meditating, regardless of how you feel. It can very valuable and important to sit through the hindrances. At other times it is more skillful to let go of any preconceived form, maybe going for a walk or reading instead. This is different from just following your likes and dislikes. I suggest experimenting with both approaches. If the equanimity and awareness is strong, then it does not matter what the form looks like. Just live in the flow of your experience with a mind of nonclinging. Let your inner teacher be your guide and look honestly at the results. That will inform you what is needed next.

Ease and Relaxation

It can feel especially demanding when first starting out if you are restless and it is hard to sit still, or if you keep falling asleep, or your body is not used to the sitting posture and hurts. Perhaps you can only manage one or two mindful breaths before becoming so deeply lost in thought that you completely forget about being with the breath for the next ten minutes. The typical untrained mind is out

21

of control; just at the time when we are the least settled, calm, or peaceful, and when we could use a lot of concentration and stability to help us be present with all these difficulties, we have these qualities the least.

Recognize that it takes practice and training for the mind to begin to settle and, just as with any art or skill, we are not going to become expert meditators in a single day. Proficiency and ability develop over time, yet many of us sit down to meditate and expect our minds to be quiet and peaceful right away. It should not surprise us that meditation can be challenging in the beginning. Our minds are not trained. Reflect on how much time you have spent on automatic pilot, led around by your likes and dislikes with a distracted mind. That is a lot of time training your mind to be scattered and not present.

Ajahn Chah, the great Thai meditation master, compared meditation practice with growing a chili bush. He said our job is to prepare the soil, plant the seed, water it, and protect it from insects. That is our whole job. We do our part, and after that how fast or in what manner it grows is not our business. You cannot pull on the leaves and expect them to grow. Yet in meditation we expect the plant to grow, flower, and produce chilies in one day.

All you can do is aim yourself in the right direction. How meditation unfolds, how quickly and in what way, is not within your control. Here is where the quality of patience will serve to support you very well. Your job is to practice the best you can, connecting with whatever experience the breath, body, and mind are giving you. You do not have to be better at meditation than you are, and that includes your capacity to let the process unfold and reveal itself in its own way. Patience and the wisdom to not suffer are among the skills you are cultivating by doing your best to let go of struggle and relax into your experience.

Ease and relaxation are foundational to meditation practice. We cannot even begin to settle if we are struggling. Consciously beginning by bringing in a sense of relaxation and ease, just the best you can, will help you let go of constriction and tension and take the striving out of the process.

Opening to the Present Moment

Meditation practice is an exploration, a process of recognizing and fostering what is skillful and learning to let go of what is unskillful. If our practice is about learning, then we are not afraid of anything that might happen. We need not worry because whatever happens is teaching us. If we regard every experience as a teacher, we can apply ourselves with an attitude of experiment and inquiry, not judging our meditation in terms of how concentrated we are, as so many of us do, but with interest to find out what is real and true.

We can be curious, doing the best we can to meet our experience with inquisitiveness and look to see if what we are doing is helpful or unhelpful. What we learn we can apply to the next situation. Even falling into struggle is an opportunity for learning; it helps you to realize that you are unable to be equanimous in this situation. Instead of floundering in self-judgment or criticism, merely look to see what happened. Any time you discover an edge—those things, situations, and experiences you feel you cannot be with—important areas for growth are revealed. Whatever happened is teaching you, giving you information, informing you how to move forward.

A big shift came in my own practice when I got just as interested in my suffering as I was in my bliss. As my mind became less distracted, I could see more and more clearly every time something unpleasant or painful would arise and how my mind responded. I began to stop worrying about whether or not I was getting what I wanted and turned to my experience with an attitude of interest and investigation.

Let your experience of the moment be your teacher. See if you can turn directly to meet whatever is happening, even if it is painful.

That does not mean you have to stay with it, making yourself plunge into something difficult, scary, or distressing, if it is too much for you. You have to look and see what is needed, letting however much skill, experience, and wisdom you have show you the way. It may be that you choose to stay right in the fire of an uncomfortable feeling, emotion, or memory, or you may back away, bringing down the intensity to get some relief in order to give you the rest and resources you need.

If you are judging yourself or your experience, try your best to stop. Do not make it a struggle to stop struggling, but try to let it go as best you can. Sometimes it is not so easy, in which case you are learning something about conditioned patterns of tension and stress that may be deeply habituated. You may need to inquire and investigate what is fueling the tendency to hold on to some painful reaction even when you see that it is creating more suffering.

Relaxation, ease, and patience will be your allies as you learn to let go of struggle and begin to meet yourself with kindness, compassion, and a sense of exploration and experimentation. Your practice is to study and learn about yourself, and nothing need be excluded. Everything is an opportunity for learning.

We tend to judge our meditation by how pleasant or unpleasant it is. When the practice is to our liking, when it feels good and we are getting what we want, we call that a good meditation. When the present moment is not how you have decided it should be, when it seems to go badly or fall apart, check to see what you have found out about yourself, about how your mind works and about the places you get stuck. See if there is something you can let go of that is unhelpful. How can you build on what you have learned? If you can let go of judgment and contention, shifting your attitude from always seeking what you want and avoiding what you do not want, you can begin looking at what happens with interest, discerning what you can cultivate that is skillful and what is unskillful that you can let go.

In the late sixties and early seventies it was common to see posters around the San Francisco Bay Area of the Indian guru Meher Baba, with his big grin and bushy mustache and the simple caption: "Don't worry, be happy." That was in the early days of my meditation practice; I remember thinking that it was a nice sentiment, like something you might say to children, but not really all that deep. It was only much later that I was able to appreciate Meher Baba's deceptively simple teaching. As you reflect on your meditation practice and how it is going, take a few moments right now to let the words soak in and notice however they land for you: "Don't worry." "Be happy."

In beginning any practice it is helpful to try to let go of expectations. Of course, we would not take up a practice if we did not expect some results. But results come more quickly, and with less suffering, if you can practice in a way that allows you to be at peace and happy where you are, even as you aim toward a goal. Be as happy and relaxed as you can. Find the freedom in the moment while practicing in a way that heads in a skillful direction.

Sometimes it may feel like you are working very hard, but even in those times you can learn to rest and relax. Check if there is any tension or constriction in your body. Try to relax those areas. Do you find some sense that you have got to change your experience? See if you can let that go and relax into whatever is happening. This is Right Effort, being fully in the present while naturally heading toward more peace, clarity, and awareness, getting somewhere and going nowhere.

After a few months on one long retreat I complained to the teacher that I had not yet reached jhana, which I had previously attained by this point. At that time I had already been meditating for more than thirty years, having sat many retreats of various lengths along with a strong daily practice. I had attained jhana in about four or five weeks of intensive meditation, so going into this retreat I thought, *This is going to be great! I'll be in jhana in a month or two at the most, and then proceed from there to even deeper stages of concentration, insight, and liberation.*

The teacher asked if I could be perfectly happy and at ease if I never attained jhana again, and kindly pointed out that real freedom is found not in attainments, but in nonclinging to whatever is happening. I remember answering with something like, "Yes, of course that is true, but in order to deeply realize that fact I've got to get..." and then proceeding to suffer and struggle for some time more. I'd had it all planned out. I knew that any time the thought *I've got to get* comes up about anything, it is a setup for suffering. But what had been a wholesome aspiration had become hijacked by my greedy mind.

All the parts of yourself and all the patterns at work in your life come with you as you begin to meditate. Just as we are liable to suffer when we do not get what we want in the course of daily life, even with the most sincere intentions we can fall into worry, stress, or fear as the meditation process unfolds. This is all part of the learning process as we get to see how our minds work. You do not have to be free from patterns of negativity in order to begin meditation, but you do need the tools to work with whatever meditation presents.

Working with Hindrances

You cannot meditate without any problems or difficulties ever arising. From time to time all of us will be troubled by sleepiness, restlessness, worry, desire, aversion, or doubt, and we need to find ways to navigate these challenges when they assail our minds.

When engaging in any form of meditation, mindfulness is the way to deal with these hindrances effectively. Often we cannot simply concentrate or focus our minds to push through problems. Through meditation we are cultivating a stable, clear awareness that bolsters our inner resources to meet these hindrances. When concentration is strong and our minds are settled, there are not so many distractions, and if unpleasant experiences do arise they do not bother us. When concentration is quite strong the hindrances cannot arise at all. Concentration suppresses the hindrances, but until it is well developed we need to find ways to set the hindrances aside enough to be able to get into concentration and jhana. When the concentration is not strong there is a range of skillful means, various approaches and techniques, for dealing with hindrances.

Often just being mindful that a hindrance has arisen is enough to loosen its grip and enable us to let it go. Experiences become hindrances only when they are stronger than our ability to meet them with equanimity. There is something about their quality that catches our minds; they become problems that we tend to struggle with and get caught in. When we are mindful and clearly aware of what is happening, we are often able to meet the same challenges with a calm, nonreactive presence.

Sometimes mindfulness alone will not be enough to enable us to act effectively when we encounter problems. At such times we must find other ways to work with them. We may need to find ways to bring down their intensity if they are too strong for us, or to suppress them or let them go.

Antidotes are ways of directing our attention in order to release a hindrance or have it fade away. If we are holding on to something pleasant, sometimes reflecting on impermanence—reminding ourselves that this experience will not last—can help us let it go. Conversely, if we are aware of something unpleasant and are experiencing aversion, perhaps consciously bringing some loving-kindness to the situation, to ourselves, or to whatever the object is can help.

In dealing with sloth and torpor we can look for ways to increase our energy. You may need more rest—a nap could help. Or try standing up during the meditation; open your eyes and take some deeper breaths. If you are restless, with your mind scattered and unable to focus, try bringing up the effort more. Or you may need to take a walk or do some other kind of movement to help get the excess energy out.

Doubt, which can be the most insidious of the hindrances, colors our perception and undermines our ability to discern that a hindrance has arisen. We are liable to become identified with the doubt, believing our thoughts that the practice does not work or that we cannot do it. We may need to talk with a friend or teacher to get a more objective perspective; or to spend time with a dharma community (whether in person or with a "virtual community" online); or to read inspiring books or listen to talks. Find whatever supports you.

Hindrances are going to happen for all of us. When they attack and are quite strong, and you have tried various strategies and nothing seems to work, your practice will be to know that that is the way it is for you. Sometimes the best we can do is bring some compassion to ourselves for all the times we get caught up in struggle or forget.

Self-Compassion

I remember my beginning days as a meditator, wondering what it was going to be like if something ever started to happen. I was young, naïve, and idealistic, and looking around the meditation hall, seeing everyone sitting so still, looking like perfect Buddhas, I thought, *Look at them all. Everybody is blissed out but me.* I imagined everyone in transcendent states of ecstasy as I grappled with knee pain, a mind that could not stay on the breath, and thoughts of inadequacy. It is so easy to fall into judging ourselves and comparing with others, and we can end up creating a lot of unnecessary suffering along this path whose purpose is to take us to the end of suffering.

It is often taught that morality is the foundation for beginning any meditation practice. Morality entails speaking, thinking, and acting in wholesome ways that decrease stress and increase well-being in ourselves and others. A standard Buddhist model to guide us in this way is the five precepts: nonharming, not stealing or not taking that which does not belong to us, care not to cause harm around sexuality, wise and careful speech, and abstaining from intoxication that leads to heedlessness. There is no doubt of the critical importance a moral basis has in creating a healthy and supportive environment for our meditation to flourish.

But even more fundamental than morality is self-compassion. Self-compassion understands that we each have our own suffering, that each of us is a unique blend of strengths and weaknesses, and it allows us to be present with our suffering without adding negative self-judgment or blame.

We see how simple the instructions for beginning meditation are. Make yourself as comfortable as possible. Sit any way you wish that will allow you to remain relatively still in a relaxed way (you can even lie down). You do not have to make anything happen, but just be mindful of whatever *is* happening. Yet we soon discover how difficult this simple process can be.

Some amount of physical and mental discomfort inevitably comes when we set aside our usual distractions and concerns to just sit quietly and be present with ourselves. Our bodies ache, or our feelings—of unworthiness, shame, fear, guilt, trying to please others, or any of the many other psychological and emotional difficulties so many of us contend with—can come roaring up at any time.

We can be quite critical or judgmental, thinking that we really are not doing any of this very well and falling into adversarial relationships with our experience and ourselves. When difficulties arise we tend to think something is going wrong, or that we are not trying hard enough or are not doing it the right way. But if you could meditate better you would. If you could concentrate better you would. If you could be less distracted or meditate more often, then you would.

Self-compassion allows us relax more, to understand that we are trying our best (even though it may not feel that way to us), that the forces that distract us or pull us to waste time are very real, and that sometimes, despite our best efforts, we do not get the results we want.

We do not have to know how to have self-compassion; we just have to be open to the possibility of self-compassion, learning to stay present to our experience with an open heart without judgment or blame. Even in the beginning we can start to bring equanimity toward our experience and our self.

Experimental Attitude

A skilled carpenter never reaches for a hammer when he needs to tighten a screw; he works seamlessly and with ease with whatever situation is presented. He doesn't fret or judge that the screw is not a nail, but concerns himself with completing his job well. We need a range of skillful means at our disposal, adding many tools to our tool kit over time and with experience, and learning how to use them confidently and effectively. Instead of feeling oppressed by a situation, complaining when things are not going our way and struggling against ourselves, we can avoid a lot of stress by letting go of our ideas of how things should be and turning with interest to meet whatever our meditation is presenting us.

By attending directly to whatever is happening, your experience will tell you what is needed and how to proceed. If you become stuck in a fixed idea of what is supposed to happen when you sit to meditate, you can fall into a struggle with your experience and yourself. Becoming a skilled meditator means learning to meet even challenging situations with interest and curiosity. We can get just as interested in our struggles and sufferings as we can in our bliss. Sometimes we will want to investigate the situation, verbally or nonverbally. Sometimes all we need is to be present and wait as the situation unfolds.

Meditation, therefore, involves a degree of experimentation, trial and error, engaging in the practice and seeing what actually happens, not seeking some prescribed set of experiences we are told should happen. Whatever happens really is just fine. Even when things seem to go wrong, the present moment is giving us information, informing us how to proceed in the next step.

All you have to do is stay open and receptive to what your experience is telling you. When your mind is steady and clear and nothing else is calling for your attention, continue cultivating the concentration. There will be plenty of times when you cannot concentrate or you are dealing with other experiences or you just sense that you should turn toward and investigate what is happening in some way. At those times, simply follow out the investigation without worrying about concentration, working as skillfully as you can with whatever the moment brings. In this way, you never have to choose between when to do concentration and when to do insight practice, and you can take both as far and deep as you wish.

As meditation progresses the instructions will begin to differ for each of us, depending not only on what happens, but also on what we are learning about our strengths and challenges in working with those experiences. When the practice is difficult or painful, we work skillfully with the pain. When the mind is calm, collected, and concentrated, we work skillfully with the pleasure.

Bringing an open, receptive attitude will be a tremendous support in deepening your capacity for working with the unfolding stages of meditation. The receptive attitude is not afraid of anything that might happen. It only looks to see what actually is happening and how we can work with it most skillfully.

Think of each meditation practice as a doorway into the same inner sanctuary. We do not want to become preoccupied with a particular door, thinking ours is the best or the only way—there can be many. It does not matter which you choose. Once you have stepped through that doorway you will guide and steer the practices so they begin to converge at one place, which is a synthesis and integration of concentration and insight. How we get there will differ from one person to the next, because each practice can bring its own result and the experiences each of us have, even if we are all doing the same practice, will vary. So at each stage I will offer a range of techniques and possible ways to work with each practice in order to head them in the same direction. I will offer various practices you might try, starting with mindfulness of breathing meditation. Through experimentation and experience, along with the guidance presented here, you will find what quiets your mind and opens your heart, what brightens mindful awareness and deepens connection with your body and mind.

You will learn to meditate so the mind becomes more collected and centered, leading ultimately to the deepest stages of concentration. At the same time, you will be guided so that mindfulness and clear awareness of all experiences are strengthened, regardless of the level of concentration present—so that insight can flourish. Awareness will be guided to open into mindfulness of your body and of the states of your heart and mind, revealing and deeply connecting with all aspects of your experience.

Ultimately, you must rely on your intuition and best judgment on how to proceed. You engage in some meditation practice to which you are drawn, or which you are taught by a teacher you happen to encounter or read about in books, and then you undertake that practice to the best of your ability and assess the results as best you can. With time and experience you will come to know what you can trust. But in order to learn how to rely on your own inner guidance you have to try out the instructions, put them into practice, and see what the results are.

Chapter 2

BEGINNING INSTRUCTIONS

It can be helpful to establish an environment that is relatively free from distraction. As your meditation practice develops and your ability to calm your mind and remain mindfully present strengthens, it will not matter when or where you choose to practice. You will be able to meditate in any situation. Especially in the beginning, though, finding a time and place relatively free from noise or commotion can be a great support.

Pick any place you like to sit quietly for the duration of the meditation period. It does not have to be perfectly quiet. Just do the best you can with whatever situation you have to work with. You can meditate at any time of day, early in the morning, late at night, or during a lunch break—whenever feels best and your schedule will allow.

Perhaps turning off your phone will support you to let go of thinking about messages or other distractions. Some people use a timer to end the sitting period so they do not have to think about when to end. It is okay to use a clock, but be careful not to fall into peeking at the time too often. Or you can meditate without timing the period at all, simply sitting however long you wish. See what works best to help you be more fully present for the meditation.

When the meditation period is over, you can get up whenever you feel ready. You may want to remain sitting a short while to reconnect with and transition to your surroundings. Sometimes this helps to carry the meditative awareness back to your ordinary activities. Or you can get up right away.

We will begin with the simple practice of mindfulness of breathing, connecting with our experience of the breath wherever in the body we can feel it most easily and clearly. We will pay attention to how the practice unfolds, using whatever actually happens to inform what is needed at the next step.

It may be obvious that mindfulness of breathing is a good fit for you or it may not be clear or easy to figure out. Give it some time. Just because you cannot concentrate well on your breath does not mean it is not a good meditation subject for you to work with. Often, it simply means that your mind is not yet trained, so do not be too quick to give up on the breath and switch to something else. What happens as we meditate will be different for each of us, and we each have our own strengths and ways of working.

If, after trying out mindfulness of breathing for a while, you feel drawn to one of the subsequent practices I offer, feel free to give it a try. Mindfulness of breathing is not the best practice for everyone. Find a style of meditation that you feel drawn to do.

Mindfulness of Breathing: Our Foundational Meditation Practice

Begin meditation practice very simply, with mindfulness of breathing, by resting your attention at some place in the body where you can feel your breathing easily and clearly. The breath is our teacher; we are learning how to be present with something as we connect mindfully with the experience of breathing just as it is happening now.

Sit in a way that is relaxed and upright with as much ease and comfort as possible, finding the balance between not straining to sit straight and not slumping. Your posture does not have to be very formal; you can be in a chair, or in a cross-legged position on a cushion, or on a meditation bench on the floor. If you have back problems you could even lie down as long as you are able to stay alert and not get sleepy.

If you are new to meditation it may require some experimentation to find a posture that best supports you to sit for the duration of the meditation period with as little pain as possible. Our bodies will not allow some of us to be comfortable regardless of the position we choose, so just do the best you can to find a posture that will allow you to sit quietly without moving too often.

Let your eyes close in a relaxed way and take a few moments to feel your body sitting. Notice that you do not have to do much and that the experience of your body, in whatever position it is in, is easily known just by paying attention in this very simple way. Some people think meditation is complicated or mysterious, but the foundation of our entire practice is simply opening to, and mindfully connecting with, our experience in order to meet each moment just as it presents itself.

Bring your awareness to your body breathing. As you pay attention to your body, you can become aware of your breathing in a simple, uncomplicated way. This is not thinking about your breathing or analyzing it, but just resting your attention on the direct, bare experience. Try to let go of your judgments or opinions—*This breath is not clear enough, This is not right breathing*—and see how you can become more receptive to the pure simplicity of each breath.

Check in with your body to see where you naturally and most clearly feel the physical sensations of breathing. It could be at the nose, in the abdomen, or whole-body breathing—all are part of the body. Give emphasis to mindfulness of breathing, letting other experiences stay in the background of your awareness as much as possible without struggling to do so. Try not to control the breath, but let the body breathe at its own rhythm. We are not trying to make the breath be any special way. The body knows how to breathe all on its own, breathing itself without you having to make it happen.

Find where your attention naturally wants to settle and stay with that. We do not want to be jumping around from one place to another. It does not matter where in the body you connect with your breathing. All places work equally well to cultivate even the deepest stages of concentration and insight; the key is to find the place where you naturally feel your breathing most clearly and easily, without strain. If you do not have an obvious preference, try bringing your attention to the area of your nose, feeling the air going in and out. For some people, concentration strengthens more quickly and sharply by focusing their attention there, though that is not true for everyone.

Later, as your meditation evolves and concentration deepens, your awareness may naturally be drawn on its own to other areas in your body. When that happens, don't fight yourself, but simply follow your experience, let it unfold and present itself to you. This is not jumping around, but is following the organic progression. For now, keep it simple and stay with your breathing in one place.

Do not move your attention to follow the breath from the nose down into the chest and back up. Being mindful of breathing at the nose is sometimes likened to a saw cutting wood. The saw's long blade moves back and forth, but only touches the log at one place. Air moves from the outside to deep in the lungs; though it "touches" the body in more than one place, we do not follow it with our attention from the nose down into the lungs. Let your awareness rest at one place, either just inside the nostrils or anywhere deeper inside the nasal passage area. Try it out and let your attention fall wherever in the area of the nose you naturally feel the breath.

You may feel your body breathing most clearly by noticing the rising and falling of your abdomen. In this case you are not feeling the sensation of air, but the physical movement of your belly expanding and contracting with each in-breath and out-breath. Again, let your body breathe at its own pace, as deeply or shallowly as it wishes, and let your awareness rest on the physical sensations of the belly rising and falling.

Variation: Whole-Body Breathing

Another way to practice is called "whole-body" breathing. This does not mean trying to feel the breath everywhere in your body, including the arms and legs, but entails widening your mindful awareness to include the experience of breathing at the nose, chest, and abdomen—the whole torso all at once, rather than focusing narrowly just at the nose or the abdomen. You may not feel your breathing in all these places, and it is fine if you notice the breath at some places in your body but not at others. For example, you may feel breathing at your chest and abdomen but not the nose. Let the sensations of breath present themselves to you naturally, not trying to make yourself feel them in any particular way.

It may be immediately obvious where you feel your breath best or you may need to experiment, spending some time following your breathing at each of these places. If you are not sure, just pick one of these styles and stick with it for a while to see how well it works.

Later we will talk about working with all the other experiences that can arise—the range of body sensations, sounds, thoughts, and moods that pull our attention and that can make it hard to stay with the breath. For now, give emphasis to awareness of the breath, not clinging to it or pushing away any other experiences, just with a strong preference for that particular awareness while letting other experiences remain in the background. Stay relaxed the best you can.

Continue practicing in this way, returning to the physical experience of breathing over and over again. In the following chapters we will talk about some of the common ways meditation can unfold and how to work with our experience in each case. For now, just stay with your breath in a simple way. Later, as the practice unfolds, we will pay attention to what happens, which will inform the next steps. As we emphasized in the previous chapter, there is no one-size-fits-all instruction for what to do next. We will not know until we see how the practice unfolds and what actually happens.

When the Mind Wanders

At any time, but especially in the early stages of practice when our minds are not trained, the mind can have a tendency to wander away in thoughts of planning, worry, or fantasy, completely forgetting to be with the breath. This is to be expected; it's the nature of an untrained mind. One of the first insights we have is the realization of how out of control our minds are.

You cannot stop your mind from wandering. Such wandering is natural and it will happen many, many times. Remember to stay relaxed and do not struggle to remain present and connected. Once you realize you have forgotten about your breath you are already back, so just start again and stay with your breathing the best you can. Meditation is a process of returning over and over, each time you drift away. Try not to create a problem or beat yourself up because you have wandered away again.

Mental Noting

You can try experimenting with mental noting, an aid that helps direct the attention to remain present with the breath. Some people find this technique very helpful to stay more connected and consistent with mindful breathing and not wander off so much, while others find it unhelpful or unwieldy. If the latter is the case with you, just let it go and continue simply with the bare experience of breathing.

Mentally repeat the words *in* and *out* with each in-breath and out-breath, keeping most of your attention on the sensation of breathing itself and letting the words remain soft and in the background of your awareness. If you are mindful of your breathing at the abdomen, you can use the words *rising* and *falling* with each rise and fall of your belly, or simply *breathing, breathing*, with each whole-body in-breath and out-breath.

Mala

Just as mental noting is an internal aid, a mala is an external aid to help keep the breath in mind. The mala is a string of beads of any size and length that is comfortable to pass between your thumb and any other finger. If you use a mala as an accompaniment to breathing meditation, a single bead marks each complete in-and-out breath cycle. Place your thumb on the bead with the in-breath and pull it across your finger with the out-breath. Just as with mental noting, you may or may not find the mala helpful to stay more present with the breath.

Breathing, mental noting, and the mala can all be used together, giving your mind three things to do at once, all pointing toward one thing, mindfulness of breathing. You can coordinate mental noting and the tactile experience of moving the beads by grabbing the bead with the *in* note and pulling it across your finger with the *out*, always keeping the physical experience of breathing foremost in your awareness.

These props, mental noting and the mala, will begin to feel cumbersome at some point as your concentration strengthens. The very supports that you may have found so helpful early on will have done their job and you will need, and want, to let them go. Feel free to use them as much as you like for now, especially when you need lots of support, but be watchful to not become attached or reliant after their useful time has passed.

Alternative Meditation Practices

The breath is commonly taught as a universal meditation subject, suitable for everyone. But for some people the breath is not a good object to work with. I knew a man who had a choking incident as a child, and paying attention to his breathing brought up feelings of anxiety. Another person with asthma found that she became tense whenever she focused on the breath. If you are one for whom the breath does not work well, there is nothing wrong; this will not hinder your ability to meditate. It's just a matter of finding the right practice in these early stages to substitute for breath meditation.

Here are some techniques you can try if you think mindfulness of breathing is not a good practice for you. These common alternatives are not the only methods that can substitute for mindful breathing, but the full range of possibilities is beyond our scope here.

Mindfulness of Sound

In the instructions for mindfulness of breathing we let all other experiences stay in the background of our awareness, not forcing or pushing them away but bringing a gentle sense of allowing them to be in the background while giving some preference or predominance to awareness of our breathing. In the same way, with this practice we allow other experiences to stay in the background and we give preference or predominance to the experience of sound. You may feel a natural draw or pull to awareness of hearing, and this practice can be very calming and settling. Those for whom mindfulness of sound works well commonly report it as an easily accessible and even compelling meditation object. You may be drawn to awareness of the sounds themselves or you may be more naturally aware of the act or the process of listening or hearing.

Mindfulness of sound entails working with either inner or outer sound. Even though it may be very quiet where you are meditating, you may feel drawn to rest your awareness in listening to however many or few sounds may be present at any time. Other people hear an inner sound: a clear perception of ringing or some other sound, experienced not through the ears but in the mind. You can see if you have such an experience and if you are drawn to rest in awareness of inner or outer sound.

If you are working with mental noting, you can mentally repeat *hearing* or *sound* if that helps you stay connected and centered with the auditory experience. If you practice mindfulness of sound, just substitute *hearing* every time I use the terms *breath* or *breathing*.

Touch Points

Pick a few places in your body—touch points through which you cycle your attention. They can be any place. For example, you could choose the feeling of your hands touching together or wherever they are resting on your thighs or knees, the feeling of your lips touching, and the feeling of your bottom pressing against the chair, cushion, or bench. It does not matter where in your body you choose, as long as they are places where you can feel some sensation easily and clearly.

Place your attention at one of these points and rest it there for a few moments, however long you wish—maybe as long as two, three, or five breaths—making a mental note of *touching, touching* if you are using noting. When you are ready, move your attention to the next place, and then the next, continuing to cycle through your touch points in this way. You do not have to bring awareness of breathing into the process, though you can if you wish. If so, experiment with how awareness of breathing can help deepen your connection with touch points.

Body Scan

Body scan involves sweeping your attention systematically through your body, generally moving down through your body (though you can move up if that is more natural for you) and placing your awareness at each place for a few seconds or longer. As you move your attention through your body, you may have a lot of sensation at a particular place or just a general sense of having your attention there without any particular sensation being noticeable.

For example, if you start at the top of your head, rest your awareness there and when you are ready slowly move your attention down through your head. You could spend a lot of time, going into detail, putting your attention into many parts of your face, the back of your head, the sides, and so on; or just experience a general sense of moving your awareness through your head without spending time in so many detailed places.

When you are ready, finding your natural pace, continue moving your awareness slowly through your head, neck, and down into your shoulders, paying attention to each place in as much or as little detail as you wish. You may or may not put your awareness individually down through the arms. Continue in this way down through your torso, possibly in your chest or back or just a general sense through your torso, and so on, moving your awareness all the way down through your legs and into your feet. When you are ready, start again, move your attention back to the top of your head and repeat the body-scanning process throughout your meditation session.

Mantra Meditation

Mantra meditation involves choosing some word, sound, or phrase that is repeated mentally over and over again. The words or phrases may or may not have meaning. You may have heard mantras chanted out loud, but as we are teaching here, all mantras should only be repeated mentally. In this way of practice, just as with the breath or sound, give strong preference to repeating the mantra and let all other experiences stay in the background.

This is a very powerful, concentrating practice if it is the right practice for you. You may already know some mantras you want to try, or you could just pick something now. For example, you could pick the name of the Buddha, and repeat *Buddha, Buddha*, over and over again. And, while it is not necessary, you could coordinate the mantra with your breathing, repeating *Bud* on the in-breath and *dha* on the out-breath, and similarly for any other mantra you might be working with. You can use a mala to help you stay present and connected with the mantra, whether or not you coordinate the mantra with your breathing.

An example of mantra practice is the way that *metta* (lovingkindness) meditation is often taught, which is through the use of phrases of loving-kindness. Pick one, two, or three phrases of lovingkindness, which could be directing loving-kindness to yourself or to others. For example, you could repeat *May I be happy* or *May you be happy* or *May you be peaceful* or *May you be safe*. These are just some examples of phrases of loving-kindness; you can make up your own. Repeat the phrases over and over, rotating through them one by one, and this mantra repetition can become the foundation for your meditation. Let that be the vehicle to take you into deeper states of concentration.

Practicing metta in this way brings all the concentration power that repeating mantras offers, but because the phrases have meaning, that meaning comes in and becomes extra empowered through the use of the mantra.

As you begin to work with any of these practices, try to incorporate a feeling of balance and ease into your meditation. For now, do not worry about anything else except establishing a connection, a relationship, with your primary practice—breath, sound, body scan, touch points, or mantra. Gently bring your attention back, over and over, to reconnect when your attention has wandered away.

In the coming chapters you will learn to practice so that mindfulness, insight, and concentration are integrated. We are not only learning to flow seamlessly between concentration and insight, we will bring insight into even the deep states of concentration. Mindfulness comes up to meet whatever level of concentration you have, so that awareness of the body, mind, and heart is retained and the opportunity for insight is never lost. In this way insight meditation is right there along with the concentration.

A steady, undistracted awareness that lets us see when we really are resting at peace within the ever-changing experience of our life is the goal of a balanced and unified practice. Without chasing after or pushing away anything, and doing nothing that takes you away from yourself or out of your experience, aim toward clarity and calm. Let every experience be your teacher.

Chapter 3

As Concentration Begins to Grow

A t some point you will begin to experience the first "aha" moments of meditation, as concentration begins to strengthen, as undistractedness deepens and grows. It may only be for short periods, but sooner or later there will be a noticeable shift in your consciousness. The change may be slight in the beginning, but you will clearly feel calmer, more peaceful or still, perhaps in ways you have never touched before.

As you hear this, be careful not to fall into comparing or judging your meditation or yourself if your mind is not settling down and you are still waiting to taste some of these experiences. Maybe you are wondering if anything is ever going to happen for you. Try to relax and let things unfold in their own time.

You do not want to chase after some experience you think you are supposed to have or to fall into struggle trying to have someone else's experience. Do not try to make anything happen, but be mindful about whatever actually is happening. What is important, and what to get interested in, is your own experience, the unique expression of how meditation unfolds for you—and that includes not yet noticing any effects from your efforts.

The unfolding of meditation can express itself in lots of ways. How is it you know you are starting to concentrate and to settle more deeply into the meditation? You know because you are having some kind of experience that is telling you so. Though you will not have to wonder if meditation is deepening—it will be obvious—the progression of meditation and the many experiences that can come with it are highly individual and can vary greatly from one person to the next.

You may feel expansive, as if your body or mind has become vast and spacious. A concentrated mind can feel very pleasant and even blissful, and the pleasant sensations can be experienced in the body, or as mental phenomena, or as not clearly located any place in particular. Some people begin to experience feelings of warmth or energy moving in their body. Others see lights or images, or hear inner sounds. These sounds and images can be easily recognizable and familiar, or they may be vague and not clearly formed. For some, deepening concentration brings a wonderful heart opening, where you are filled with kindness, compassion, or love extending unconditionally to yourself and others. These are among the experiences of concentration, any of which can be dramatic and strong, or smooth and light.

By now you have no doubt seen how hard it can be simply to sit quietly with yourself. If your mind is spinning out of control, you may have wondered, *What is the point of all this?* When you feel restless or your body aches, it can take real commitment to stay with the practice. Challenges can arise any time in meditation, but it can be especially difficult when we do not have the support of a clear, steady mind.

Now you gain confidence that the practice works and that you can really do it. The building momentum starts to do some of the work for you, strengthening and sustaining your ability to meet whatever might happen. It feels like more of the practice is happening on its own and you don't have to put in so much effort to make it happen.

Sustained and encouraged by these initial experiences, you will begin to feel closer, more familiar with your breathing. Where perhaps you were bored or restless, now you can be interested. What is this breath? Where is the deepening process leading? Now is the time to begin discovering how your practice can be more intimate, letting the felt sense, the nonconceptual experiential knowing of the breath, strengthen and grow.

See how long you can stay present and aware of the whole breath. Connect with the full cycle of breath, feeling the beginning, staying with it in the middle and through to the end. Notice the pause before the beginning of the out-breath and stay with that all the way to the pause before the next in-breath. Experiment and explore how you can be even more fully in contact, more fully immersed in the sensations of your breathing, letting it capture your attention and fill your awareness.

As meditation progresses, our practice can begin to shift and reveal itself to us in new ways. We must be ready to let go of how things have been, and open to how the moment is presenting itself with fresh interest and curiosity.

Foreground and Background

Sometimes, without your doing anything to make it happen, you will feel the concentration experiences more strongly than the breath. You will be more clearly aware of the peace, the stillness, the expansiveness, the energies, or the pleasantness than you are of the sensations of breathing. Whatever your concentration experiences are, they are naturally predominating and popping out to your awareness, even though you can still clearly feel the physical experience of your breath, or whatever other meditation practice you may be doing. When that happens, if that happens, you do not have to do anything about it at that point. Mindfully know that that is the way the meditation is presenting itself and continue on with your practice as you have been.

At other times your experience may unfold in just the opposite way. Even though the experiences of concentration may be strong, the physical sensations of breathing become more prominent and you will feel them more easily and naturally than you will the concentration. Again, you do not have to do anything except notice that that is how the meditation is expressing itself, and continue practicing as you have been, just staying with your breathing.

Deepening meditation can manifest in a third way, where you are more or less equally aware of the experiences of concentration and the sensations of the breath, the sound, the touch points, or the mantra. Sometimes the experiences of concentration and breathing can go beyond just being equal in your awareness and begin to feel merged or mixed into one new experience that cannot easily be separated. There is no longer a clear boundary between experiences of concentration and experiences of breathing, and you open to a new blended "concentration-breath" experience. Do not worry if it is hard to conceive what this blended experience might be like—it will be obvious to you if it happens. The goal is not to make this happen, but if it does, then let this new unified experience be the object of your meditation.

It may not be obvious how the concentration and the breath are unfolding in relation to each other, or whether you are feeling the breath or the concentration more strongly. It is not important to figure it out. Do not stir up your mind looking for it or get too involved in figuring out what is happening. If you are not aware of it naturally, check in now and then, perhaps a couple of times during a sitting period. But mostly simply continue with the practice of mindful breathing.

Broadening and Narrowing the Lens of Awareness

Like a camera lens zooming in and out, our awareness can expand and contract. Sometimes your awareness may feel very narrowly focused. All your attention will center on the breath and you will not pay much attention to other things going on around you. At other times your mind may be quite open and spacious, allowing other body sensations, thoughts, emotions, and sounds to be known along with the breath. And sometimes you may not have a clear sense of your awareness being either narrow or broad.

When your awareness narrows, you may not notice much else outside the meditation subject. If you are connecting with your breathing at the nose, for example, it can feel like you are concentrated in just this area, without noticing much else beyond. Other times you can feel just the opposite, like awareness is more open and inclusive of a broad range of experiences. The lens has been widened. Even though you may still be quite concentrated on the breath, there is also a broader awareness around the main meditation object.

This feeling of being narrowly or broadly focused can happen on its own, but you can also choose to narrow or widen your attention, moving in whichever direction helps you remain present and connected. It is fine to experiment some and get to know the different flavors. There is not a right or wrong setting for the lens of awareness.

Shifting Attention

So far the instructions have mainly been to keep bringing your attention back to your breath whenever your mind wanders. Continue practicing in this way, stabilizing and strengthening the connection with your breathing at the same place where you have been resting your attention all along.

The more present and undistracted your mind is, the more aware you will be of anything that happens. You can become more connected and concentrated on your breath and at the same time open increasingly to awareness of other experiences. Perception of your inner and outer world heightens and all that goes on in your body and mind is naturally known within a wider field of awareness around the central object of the breath or other primary meditation object. Any sensations in your body and experiences in your mind are easily and effortlessly known.

As you settle more deeply, your body may become very relaxed and still, so there might be less happening in your body to be aware of, but anything that does arise will clearly be known. As the progression of awareness gets even subtler, you will plainly perceive what is happening in your mind. Whatever happens, you will know it, whether your mind is contracted or expansive, concentrated or unconcentrated, grasping and clinging or equanimous and relaxed.

Do not bounce around from one place in your body to another, or from one practice to another. Practices such as body scan or touch points, which purposefully cycle through points of attention, are fine. That is not jumping around.

But you should remain receptive to the natural progression and allow the process to reveal itself in its own way. Your attention may naturally be pulled in new directions, and you should not force yourself to stay with your breath at one place if the movement elsewhere is clear and strong. Follow the natural, organic progression as the practice unfolds.

You may find that your attention wants to go to another area in your body or that something else is capturing your interest. An area you are not observing can suddenly pop out in your awareness. Sometimes you may find that the awareness naturally wants to settle on the breath at the abdomen, some days on the entire body, and some days on the nose.

Deepening concentration can move beyond the breath, manifesting in many different ways. Subtle, nonphysical sensations, such as feelings of energy, can become prominent. These kinds of experiences can open to and merge with the body, or they can become disembodied.

Do not struggle to stay with your breath where you originally started, but follow where it naturally leads. Bring a sense of experimentation and openness to see and learn where the meditation wants to take you. See what happens when you allow your awareness to follow its natural unfolding. It may stay in the new area or it may change again on its own.

If you become more agitated by allowing your attention to move, bring it back to the original object. See what results you get by following the natural progression. Look to see what disturbs your mind and what helps it settle more deeply.

If you feel restless or sleepy it is fine to shift your attention elsewhere, away from the breath to some other place in your body, or even to sound, if you find it helps. That is not jumping around. It is being skillful. It is important to find what works and what supports you best in any situation. There will always be times when we need to let go of the practice we are doing and use some other skillful means. Once you feel settled again, come back to your main practice.

More Subtle Awareness

As your awareness becomes more refined, you may begin to notice ever more subtle details of the sensations within the experience of your breathing. If you are mindful of breathing at your abdomen, you may notice the rising and falling movement in more detail, such as slight variations in pressure or whether you feel the sensations more clearly in one part of the belly than another. At the nose you may become aware that the in-breath is cool and the out-breath warmer, or begin to notice many slight shifts in sensation. You may feel tickling or notice the moving air more clearly at one place in your nose than another.

This enhanced perception of body and breath sensations can arise naturally as a fruit of meditation. It is fine if more detail and subtler experiences in the breath become apparent on their own, and that does happen for some people.

Sometimes you may choose to bring mindfulness to these subtler sensations, but in general do not go looking. Bringing this investigative attitude to the breath will strengthen concentration to a certain degree, but seeking out all the little sensations associated with your breathing is too much mental activity, too much doing, to be conducive to the deepest stages of concentration. For now, just connect with the physical sensations of breathing in a simple way and allow your experience to develop and reveal itself as it will on its own.

Building Mindfulness

A key to integrating concentration and insight is cultivating and strengthening mindfulness at every stage, from the first glimmers of steadiness and peace to the subtlest states of concentration. If you want to travel due north, you might be heading only a tiny fraction of a degree off course and not notice any difference for a long time; only once you have traveled very far will your direction really start to diverge. A very small variance in the beginning will become a very large difference over a long time, and you may end up in an entirely different place.

Your sense of direction need not be perfect. The mountain you are aiming toward comes in and out of sight many times in the course of a journey. When it is out of sight you use your best sense of direction to head roughly the right way. Once you crest the next hill and the mountain is again in plain view you can fine-tune your course.

Similarly, we are applying mindfulness in every aspect of meditation, even in little ways in the beginning, so it will strengthen and grow, coming with us as an ally and rising up to meet whatever level of concentration is there. Then it does not matter what kind of concentration we have or how strong it is, because mindfulness is always there to meet it.

The simple instructions of checking in occasionally to be aware of how the concentration experiences are unfolding in relation to the breath, or whether our attention is narrow or wide, are part of the training for bringing mindfulness and clear comprehension into the meditation process. Beginning in the earliest stages we are starting to notice what is happening. Our practice can lead in many directions and, depending on how it naturally unfolds, we may let it progress on its own or we may direct the meditation to proceed along a different path. As we become more attuned to how our practice is unfolding, we will be able to make clear choices in how we may want to steer the instructions and work with the progression of concentration and insight.

Balance

The experiences of concentration can be compelling when they are strong. It can feel very pleasant when your mind starts to calm down. When your mind settles even a little bit you begin to feel more complete and satisfied, your heart and mind nurtured and your body replenished. Meditation can become delightful, even sensual, for some people, and we tend to like it a lot. When this happens you do not have to stop liking it or deny the experience in some way. Include the pleasure you feel in meditating in your mindfulness. Continue to follow it and let it build. Notice how you feel the pleasure in your body and in your breathing. Learning how to use pleasant feelings is an important skill. Let the pleasure draw you more fully into the experience of breathing.

However, because these experiences can be so alluring, it is easy to become fascinated by them and overlook the most important part and the main reason we want to become concentrated: the undistracted awareness itself. It is especially important to distinguish between these two main aspects of a concentrated mind, the clear, steady awareness and the experiences that can happen within that awareness. In the same way that we can lose our mindfulness and get lost in whatever is happening in daily life, we can be pulled into and caught up in the happiness, peace, and pleasure of meditation. This can happen to any of us and should be viewed as another of the many situations we will encounter and learn to navigate in the life cycle of our meditation practice. Bringing attentiveness to our experience and how it unfolds starts to strengthen the mindfulness and clear awareness, which will carry into the stronger experiences of concentration we will discuss later.

Do not go after or push away any part of the breath. Stay mindful and aware, in a relaxed way, the best you can. Try not to make anything happen or to push anything away. Do not fight or get into a struggle, overstriving for some experience you want or pushing away something you don't want. We need to have the tools to work skillfully with however our meditation practice unfolds.

Chapter 4

WORKING WITH
DIFFICULTIES

Nothing proceeds in an unbroken line, just getting more and more pleasant and good without any challenges. There are always ups and downs in meditation. To practice meditation and progress, you have to acknowledge and use everything it has to offer, including the times when you cannot concentrate. You do not want to miss the opportunities for insight and growth those times provide.

Your body may ache, or painful thoughts, emotions, or memories can arise, making it difficult to sit through the experience. There will be times when you cannot concentrate and it feels like you are just sitting there waiting for the session to be over. It can be hard not to get up from meditation when you feel restless or bored, something else pulls for your attention, or you simply do not feel like doing it.

To deepen our mindfulness, concentration, and insight we need to be honest with ourselves about what is happening, employing all the skills we are learning for working with what is here, what is real, and what is true. We need an array of tools for navigating our inner landscape, the range of shifting thoughts, feelings, moods, and emotions that appear in the course of meditation—both for when our minds are clear and settled and the meditation feels pleasant and good, and when it feels like it is all falling apart.

Turning into the Skid

Formal meditation is practice for real life. All the work we put in on the meditation cushion is training ourselves to meet the moments of our life without being oppressed by them. When confronted with anything unpleasant, our habitual response is often to push it away. When our knee aches, we stretch out our leg. When old memories or feelings awaken, we distract ourselves. If we cannot concentrate, we push harder. When the present moment is not giving us what we want, we can fall into a negative reinforcing spiral of frustration, agitation, and struggle.

When negative emotions or distressing thoughts arise, we feel the affliction, even if we are mindfully present. Aches and pains are not going to melt into pleasant sensations, regardless of how we relate to them.

But we can magnify the problem by our inability to be with what is happening. A pain in our neck that will not go away is unpleasant enough. When we engage it in battle, a whole new layer of suffering is added on top of an already painful situation. We feel the pain and then add more suffering through the struggle.

When driving on icy roads, the automatic response if you begin to skid is usually to jerk the steering wheel away from the direction in which you are skidding. But to gain traction and head back in the right direction, you have to steer toward it. The way out is counterintuitive. Even if you are careening toward a building or tree, the way out is in; you have to turn into the skid. Only once you have gained traction and the tires are gripping the road can you steer away from the obstacle.

This is the challenge. We need practice so that we have the presence of mind, the space between what happens and our response to it, to choose the right course of action. Seeing the inevitable difficulties as a chance for discovery allows for the possibility of freedom. These are opportunities for taking charge of your response in any situation. The way out of suffering is not always to turn away from it, but to bring a willingness to meet your experience.

Noticing the Changing Nature

When our hearts and minds are at peace it is easy to become complacent, but clarity and ease inevitably give way to periods of difficulty and stress. Just as the sun at its zenith always sets, only to rise again, and flowers open and close according to their natural cycles, the old falls away but a fresh opportunity is left behind.

Insight begins to mature as we learn to end the struggle and turn to meet every experience as our teacher. We do not want to miss the opportunity for growth these times offer.

When hindrances arise or we do not get our way, we can learn to stop fighting ourselves. When our beautiful meditations have turned to burdens, we should not miss the potential that these times of change present to see the transitory nature of life. We begin to understand that nothing has gone wrong, that the situation has merely changed due to its own causes and conditions. This is how everything works.

Some amount of discomfort or pain is inevitable. If you sit still long enough, even if it is in a soft, comfortable chair, your body will hurt. You can lie down to meditate, or choose any posture, and eventually aches and pains will show up. We want to find the balance between shifting our posture to take care of ourselves, and letting things be and learning how to work with what is.

Knowing Your Limits

Notice your experience as you sit down to meditate. Take a few moments to settle into your sitting posture and look to see what the present moment is giving you. This is reality. What do you find is happening? It is not so much a matter of trying to be mindful of your breathing, but being interested and curious to connect with and attune yourself to whatever is actually here. Not what happened the last time you sat to meditate. The whole practice is learning how to work and be skillfully with the present, with *this* reality.

Imagine a circle, with you at the center. Inside the circle are all of the experiences you are able to be present with, whether they are pleasant or painful. Outside the circle are those situations that are too much for you to deal with, things that are so intense or difficult that you simply cannot work with them. Think of meditation practice as expanding the circle to encompass more and more of your life.

We need discernment to know what we can handle, and respect for what really is too much for us. We need to recognize where anything that happens lives in relation to our circle. The wisdom to know when to stay present with something and when, in fact, it is too much comes from experience. We will all have times when we think we are on one side of the circle and we are actually on the other. Oftentimes we struggle, moving away from pain when we really could have worked with it. When we stretch out our knee to relieve the pain or distract ourselves from some emotion, we may miss an opportunity for learning how to be present with and let go of our suffering in the face of difficulties.

There are also times when you might stay with something too long and it would have served you better to shift or move, to change the situation or bring down its intensity if you can. We think we are supposed to stay with it, believing we should be able to remain mindful and present without struggle, when in reality it is simply too much. It falls outside of our circle. We may sit with terrible knee pain, toughing it out, when we need a break—not out of aversion but out of compassion for ourselves, so that we can find some ease and our mind can relax. In those times we suffer unnecessarily.

When to stay with something and when to seek some relief is a question we all must answer for ourselves. Use your best intuition. Do not worry whether or not you made the right decision.

You do not always have the luxury of changing your circumstances, whether in meditation or in life. Whenever something really is too much, we are going to suffer if we cannot bring down the intensity or find a way out. We need a tremendous amount of compassion for ourselves in those times, when we find there is no escape from something that is beyond our learning edge. Our task then may be to bear our suffering.

You can try redirecting your attention away from the hurt toward something pleasant, safe, or comforting. While pain or sorrow may not disappear because you distract yourself, putting your mind on something pleasing can be a real support, providing a needed break and bolstering your ability to come back later with full attention to deal with the situation. We don't want to always run away from problems, but we do want to use whatever tools will help us.

Try opening your eyes and looking around for a beautiful image, perhaps a flower or painting. Feel the beauty of it. Let the pleasant feeling permeate you. Or pick up a book and read a few inspiring passages, or turn on your favorite music, finding whatever gladdens your mind and helps you feel more happy and relaxed. Notice how good it feels and consciously let the good feeling pervade your body.

Once you feel steadier and more able to meet your experience, try again, turning your attention back to work with the difficulty. Notice what is it like to meet the physical pain or emotional anguish now, and if this helps you meet the situation with some degree of nonreactive presence.

When you feel steady and clear and hindrances are not arising, stay with the breath. You may notice that your mind is quiet, your body is relaxed, and you find an ease of continuity in your attention. If you become aware that your body aches or your mind is distressed, if you are struggling, see if you can stop fighting yourself and try to let go of your suffering. Remember that we are not trying to stay with the breath and be concentrated no matter what, but we do want to stay present for and work skillfully with anything that might happen. Do not try to force yourself back to the breath when difficulties arise, but stay receptive to welcoming all experiences as part of your meditation.

Pleasant and Unpleasant

Some experiences are pleasant, some are unpleasant, and some are in between. Anything unpleasant can be hard to be with. If something is too pleasant it pulls us in, and if it is somewhere in between, neither obviously pleasant nor unpleasant, it is easy to space out or feel restless or bored. The Pali word *vedana*, commonly translated as "feeling" or "feeling tone," refers to this pleasant, unpleasant, or neutral aspect accompanying all of our experience.

Feelings act as filters to color our perceptions and influence how we relate to whatever is happening. When we are not aware of them, we tend to reactively push away anything unpleasant or to grab onto whatever is pleasant. We notice not just the experience itself, but the experience mixed with our opinions and judgments about it. If you are being mindful of knee pain in your meditation, for example, sometimes you might not notice that you are relating to the pain with some aversion. Once you have fallen into reactivity, it's much harder to let go. You want to be aware of whatever is happening, but also of the attitudes you bring to meet your experience.

Noticing the feeling tone creates a wedge of mindfulness, giving you space between what happens and your response to it. By remaining clearly aware of what is happening and the feeling tone associated with it, you can let pleasant, unpleasant, and neutral experiences all come and go without pushing away or trying to hold on to anything.

If you notice that you are tense or struggling, try checking for feeling tone. Just bringing awareness to feelings is often enough help for you to stay present with a challenging experience. You can be aware of something pleasant without holding on to it. You can know your experience is unpleasant without straining to make it go away. You can let go of indifference to meet neutral experiences with interest.

Even when your meditation seems to be going smoothly, it can be useful to check in with the feeling tone from time to time. You can notice the feeling tone of any sight, sound, smell, taste, physical sensation, or thought. Bringing such awareness to feelings can help unmask subtle areas of craving and clinging that you may not have noticed before.

Opening to All Experiences

So far we have been emphasizing letting our breathing or some other meditation object stay in the foreground and allowing all other experiences to stay in the background of our awareness. We are deepening our connection with the breath, learning to become close, familiar, and intimate with it, inclining our mind to it over other experiences. While we are cultivating a strong preference for the breath as a primary meditation subject, we will not be able to maintain that level of connection and attention all the time.

It soon becomes clear that during some days, some sittings, or some parts of sittings you will not be able to focus or stay present very well. You cannot force your mind to concentrate. You can try to force it, like prying something open that does not want to release, but that will only serve to make you more frustrated and stressed.

There are always many other experiences in addition to the main ones we are working with in meditation. At times you will find yourself agitated or restless, sleepy or dull. Your body may ache or you may be flooded with emotional pain, fear, confusion, old memories, anger, or grief. Or something else will push itself into the forefront of your consciousness, refusing to rest in the background—something with which you struggle or suffer in some way. You may be bothered by sounds or other things that previously were easy to let go and allow to remain in the background.

It can be difficult to stay present when you find yourself facing physical pain or emotional distress. At times it can be challenging not to fall into aversion when something becomes strong or compelling and you grapple and strain against what is happening.

During these times we want to find ways to open to, include, and incorporate any of these other experiences into the meditation practice. We do not want to fall into a struggle with ourselves, trying to push away whatever is happening, thinking we are supposed to stay only with our breathing.

We began learning how to be mindful by paying attention to our breathing. Then we used the breath to deepen mindfulness. The breath was our first teacher and as we continue to attend to it, mindfulness, concentration, and clear awareness all deepen, along with our ability to be present regardless of what happens. As the art and skill of meditation matures, we learn to surf the waves of all that happens, gracefully moving in a very inclusive way with the continuously changing flow of experience.

Mindfulness with Breathing

When we cannot concentrate, our back aches, or there is pain in our knee or grief in our heart, it can be hard to stay with the breath. Rather than struggling to concentrate, we can let go of the breath and stop trying to keep these difficulties at bay.

One technique to help is switching from mindfulness *of* breathing, or mindfulness of sound, to mindfulness *with* breathing, or with sound, or with any other practice you are doing. Allow the breath to come into your awareness along with whatever else you are dealing with. The breath acts as a stabilizing factor and support, helping you remain present to meet and work with the pain.

For some people it is a sense of breathing into the experience. For others, it is more a sense of having breathing in their awareness alongside whatever else is happening. It is not splitting your attention but having both together at the same time, the pain and the breathing, the emotion and the breathing. You will have to experiment and see what works best.

When meditation is easy and pleasant, breathe with it, working skillfully and wisely with the pleasure to deepen concentration. Breathe with the good feelings in your body and mind. When it is difficult, try breathing with that. The practice is not to deny or negate your pain; we are not trying to get rid of anything. If you have pain in your body, you can direct your breathing right into the pain. If you have pain in your heart, try breathing with the anger or sadness.

If you are having trouble connecting with your breathing, look to see where the block in the connection is; turn your attention to it and see if you can breathe with that. If you are unable to be with whatever that is, turn to what is stopping you *now* and see if you can breathe with *that*. Keep backing up; keep turning your attention toward whatever is keeping you from being with your present-moment experience until you find what you can be with. That is the place to focus.

Your experience will tell you what is needed and how to proceed. Notice if you are struggling, if there is some way in which you are not relaxed and at ease. Your struggle will tell you. Look to see what is going on and if you can relax into your experience. Do not fight or strain to keep the breath at the center of attention. Let go of the breath and turn with mindfulness to meet the reality of the moment.

You may need to experiment to find how you can breathe with discomfort, or how you can let the support of the sound you are working with, acting as a stabilizing influence, come in with you to meet the worry. It may not be obvious how you can breathe with strong emotion or with any other experience. Explore and experiment to find how the breath can help you be present with your distress, and incorporate it as part of the meditation. When you are not concentrated, you can breathe with that. When your back aches, you can breathe with that. You can breathe with the pain in your knee, or with your anger or grief. Let the breath help you integrate your struggles as part of the practice.

By turning toward your experience you can work with physical and emotional pain, including them in the meditation. When you are in pain or upset, if your experience is difficult or unpleasant in some way, breathe with it. Try directing the breath; see what emerges as you breathe into grief. The breath will help you remain steady and present even in the face of discomfort. It will act as a support to help you stay more relaxed.

Eventually, either in this or in a future session, things will get quieter and you will be able to concentrate again, the difficulties will subside or they will change or will not be so interesting or compelling. You will again be able to let other experiences stay in the background without struggle and you can return to the mindfulness of breathing practice.

In this way, you do not have to choose what to be aware of in your meditation. You can allow your experience to inform you. During the times when you can concentrate well, when your body is at ease and other experiences are not so strong, keep them all in the background and stay with your main, simple practice: mindfulness of breathing. At other times these experiences will become strong or you will find yourself struggling or suffering, and then you can bring in mindfulness with breathing, or with sound, letting the breathing or sound act as a support to help you stay more undistracted and present. In this way you learn to move seamlessly back and forth between mindfulness of breathing and mindfulness with breathing.

There may also be times when whatever is happening is so strong or so compelling that you just feel that you need to put your whole-hearted, full attention on the experience while letting go of the breathing completely. Even mindfulness with breathing may not be appropriate; instead, you remain fully with the other experience. During those times, too, stay with the experience until it subsides or you need a break, and whenever you choose you can come back to the home base practice of mindful breathing.

If physical or emotional pain or struggle has not settled out when it is time to end your meditation, you may wish to take the last few minutes before getting up to shift your awareness to something that helps ease the stress. If you have been sitting with body pain, change your posture. Take a few deeper breaths and stretch out your arms and legs. Open your eyes and notice your surroundings. Or you can simply get up from the session if you feel ready to transition and carry on with your day.

Over time you will learn that the course of meditation, like all of life, flows in cycles, following its own patterns and progression. You will be more able to relax with the ever-changing rhythms as they lose their power to shake you off center.

Chapter 5

RIGHT CONCENTRATION

I f you have ever undertaken the practice of bringing mindfulness into daily life, trying to be aware the best you can moment to moment and not be lost on automatic pilot, you know how hard it can be to stay present and awake. Perhaps you try to stay with your breathing or feel the movement in your feet as you move about, being mindful and clearly aware in any way you can, as much as you can. Or you use something else—feeling the phone in your hand as you talk, your hands on the steering wheel if you are driving, anything to help anchor your attention in the present moment. It is the same in meditation. Perhaps you are present for a few breaths, only to find yourself waking up sometime later from the daydream of your thoughts and worries and all the imaginings that capture your attention to remember, *Oh yeah, I forgot, I'm trying to be mindful.*

If that has ever happened to you, then you have experienced mindfulness without the support of concentration. That is a very different experience from mindfulness *with* concentration. As our practice develops, the fruits of our efforts in formal meditation permeate all the rest of our lives. We find that we are increasingly mindful naturally, without having to try to make it happen.

The Pali word we have been translating as "concentration" is *samadhi.* It is significant that the final element, the culmination, of the Eightfold Path is Right Concentration, and that the whole final section—Right Effort, Right Mindfulness, and Right Concentration—is called the samadhi group. It is not the mindfulness group; it is the concentration group.

This is telling us something. It is saying that Right Concentration includes effort, that mindfulness is included, it is not something separate, and that it includes undistractedness. All three of these elements need to work together, informing and supporting each other, in order for concentration to be Right Concentration.

It is hard to overstate the important place samadhi holds in the Buddhist path to awakening. We have to understand Right Concentration and how to apply it, especially as we begin to cultivate and attain the subtler, deeper stages in meditation. The Buddha placed great importance and emphasis on samadhi, talking about it over and over in his teachings. In addition to the prominent place samadhi holds in the Noble Eightfold Path, it is emphasized in many of the Buddhist teachings that elaborate on meditation practices.

Two Kinds of Concentration

The word "concentration" carries various connotations, each shaping how it is considered in relation to insight meditation. None of the interpretations are right or wrong, no application is better or more correct than another. I hope we can appreciate the range of ways concentration is practiced and the various ways it is related to insight so we can make conscious, informed choices in how to steer our practice, because each choice will influence the direction in which meditation unfolds in different ways.

Samadhi means "undistracted"; another good translation is "collected." An undistracted or collected mind can unfold either naturally, on its own, or by purposefully aiming in one direction or the other. Strengthening concentration can serve to connect us more intimately with our body and mind or to disconnect us from our experience.

If you continue practicing as I have been teaching here, giving emphasis to mindfulness of breathing, your ability to concentrate and remain steady and focused with the breath will grow. Your mind will progressively wander less and less and you can eventually become so skilled at centering on one thing that your mind will hardly waver at all. If you keep training your mind, taking your practice far enough, you can reach a stage in which you become extremely adept at concentrating. Your ability to remain steady and undistracted on one object will have been strengthened to the point where you will not notice any other experiences.

You will be fully engrossed, fully absorbed, just in the experience of one thing, the one meditation object, whatever it is. At this stage your mind is so fixed on a narrow point that it can never wander. At this point undistractedness has progressed to the pinnacle of steadiness.

The changing flow of experience will stop for you because your mind has become one-pointed. Ultimately, concentration can be taken so far that you will no longer notice experiences in your body, thoughts, sounds, moods, or emotions. You will lose awareness of other experiences because the ability of your mind to concentrate on this one point has been strengthened so much that your mind does not go to anything else; you do not perceive anything from any of the senses.

I call this type of undistractedness *exclusive* concentration, because the mind is exclusively focused on one thing; awareness rests exclusively on that one thing and excludes awareness of every-thing else. It is also called *one-pointedness* or *fixed concentration* because the mind can stay narrowly fixed on the one point of the breath.

The second way undistractedness can develop is equal in depth and power to one-pointed exclusive concentration, but is qualita-tively very different. In this second style of undistractedness, percep-tion of changing phenomena is never lost. Instead of being lost, your awareness of changing experiences is enhanced. At its culmination the mind itself stops, just as it does in exclusive one-pointedness, but this is stopping of a different sort.

Rather than the flow of sense perceptions stopping, the mind comes to tranquility, all the while being open, receptive, and clearly aware of the full range of changing experiences. The mind, equally still, unwavering, and steady as in one-pointedness, stops but does not stop fixed on a point.

This is a different kind of stillness, known as jhana, an utterly undistracted awareness that is open to include all that is happening.

In a later chapter we will explore the nature of jhana, and how to enter and work with those meditative states.

In order to differentiate from one-pointedness, I call this second kind of concentration *unification of mind*. This concentration is *inclusive* rather than exclusive, because it excludes nothing and is inclusive of all experiences.

The main distinction between inclusive unification of mind and exclusive one-pointed concentration is whether or not you have any experiences of changing phenomena. Exclusive concentration is disconnecting. When taken to its culmination there is no longer any sensory experience. It is a purely mental state in which the mind becomes one-pointed, such that there is only the experience of bliss, or of light, for example. All sense of changing experience is lost. You cannot experience your body.

In inclusive concentration you have not lost connection with the body; in fact, that connection is enhanced. You are aware of your body and of your mental experiences, but along with that there is a deeper place of the mind that is utterly still, clear, present, and aware. Everything is happening and unfolding within pure awareness, and the pure awareness is not moving. The mind is unmoving, mindfulness and clarity are amplified, and the connection with the whole range of your experience is heightened. It is this second style of concentration, this inclusive style, toward which we are aiming.

This distinction between two kinds of undistractedness is important as you learn to navigate the deeper, subtler stages of concentration. You may naturally incline toward unmoving focus that is concentrated exclusively on a point, losing awareness of everything else, or you may lean toward an unmoving and undistracted mind that is open and aware as all kinds of different experiences come and go. By understanding these distinctions, and with a clear sense of where you are aiming, you may choose to let the process unfold on its own, or you can steer the unfolding in either direction. In the next chapter we will discuss how to recognize in which direction you are naturally moving and how you can steer toward inclusive undistractedness, which will be a powerful support in bringing concentration and insight together.

Concentration Supports Insight

No Buddhist teachers say, "Be distracted." Everyone appreciates the importance and benefit of a clear, steady, unconfused mind for the cultivation of insight. Aiming toward more presence and stability helps you to not be lost and caught up in your thoughts, feelings, and moods. But while the ability of the mind to remain undistracted is considered important by all, there is a wide range of understandings and teachings about what that concentration should look like. Some meditation teachers de-emphasize concentration in insight meditation while others place great emphasis on its development. This can be a source of confusion, especially when reading guides like this one. If you are an experienced meditator and have heard instructions from numerous teachers, it may not be clear how, or if, these instructions fit together, or if you should be doing insight meditation or concentration practices.

In fact, you are not doing insight versus doing concentration. It is all one practice. There does not need to be any contention between mindfulness and concentration; we need not choose between the two. We can strengthen both together and aim our meditation in a way that appreciates and highlights both.

For insight and concentration to work together you have to develop the right kind of concentration. Insight necessitates an intimate connection with your entire experience so you can see what is happening and how you are relating to it. If you become too exclusively concentrated, if you lose contact with changing mental and physical experience, you lose the link with yourself and insights are not likely to arise. You will have to lift out of the concentration in order to regain awareness of the changing experiences of your body and mind and turn toward insight.

You need to stay connected with your body, heart, and mind if you want to understand their nature. Insight blossoms as you come to recognize that all things are constantly changing due to their own causes and conditions. When you try to hold on to anything that is destined to change, you sow the seeds of suffering. In order to know these truths directly, beyond ordinary intellectual understanding, you need to touch changing phenomena so that you can observe change and your responses to it. It is in service of this goal that we are cultivating unification of mind, which can go all the way to jhana without losing the experience of change. Insight can arise even in the deepest stages of samadhi; it is, in fact, enhanced since you never lose connection with change.

Since we will be developing concentration that is connecting, you are not going to lose awareness of your body and mind. Just the opposite; your connection with yourself will be enhanced. You do not have to come out of even the deepest stages of concentration into some lower level in order to do insight meditation.

You can synthesize concentration and insight into one practice through cultivation of inclusive, connecting awareness, opening whole new realms of opportunity for deepening insight. Stilling the mind to the point where you are undistracted but still connected with all experiences, you are never too concentrated. You do this by bringing up mindfulness to meet the concentration. When you have a small degree of concentration, bring the mindfulness to meet it. When concentration and its associated experiences are powerful, bring the mindfulness up to meet that. Insight is happening even in the deepest stages of concentration because you never lose connection. You can take the practice all the way to jhana and mindfulness, concentration, and insight will all come with you and be unified.

Concentration that is connecting shines a bright light of awareness with which to meet our experience in ever-subtler ways, opening the way for profound insights to arise. When concentration is connected, the ground is prepared for insights to occur both within states of concentration and without.

A Potential Pitfall of Concentration

The undistractedness that comes with being well-concentrated can generate a whole range of amazing and compelling phenomena. In a later chapter I will discuss the kinds of attractive experiences that can arise when you are concentrated—deeply satisfying feelings of peace and calm, pleasant feelings of energy moving in your body, and interesting lights and sounds. It is common for meditators to practice in order to have these experiences. The experiences of being concentrated have an important function in making the mind malleable and wieldy, and gladdening the mind, leading to relaxation and ease and allowing us to remain present with the ever-changing flow of experience.

But these pleasant experiences can be pitfalls. If meditators confuse these experiences with the greater purpose of being concentrated—to enhance awareness of and connection with our self—meditators risk becoming attached to them. We should not fear these states or try to avoid them, but should bring wisdom and discernment to working with them, just as we do with any other experience. Fear of attachment should not dissuade us from cultivating these important states of mind. If clinging to or grasping for meditative states arises, that can be a rich area for investigation and learning. Just as we should not seek after suffering, but should not fear it either, we should neither chase after the pleasures of concentration nor avoid them due to worry about attachment. I will discuss how to recognize and manage these situations. Having clear guidance, you will not have to worry about any of the experiences that might arise in your meditation.

Right Concentration

Right Concentration is always defined as the four jhanas (as we'll see, jhana is divided into four stages). If you remember that concentration really means being undistracted, then jhana is a special kind of undistracted awareness that does not leave mindfulness and insight behind. Right Concentration yokes tranquility, mindfulness, and insight evenly together.

Though the Pali texts are explicit that Right Concentration is the four jhanas, this does not mean you have wrong concentration unless you have attained jhana. Aim toward jhana but be careful not to set yourself up for overstriving. From a practice perspective it is more useful to consider Right Concentration as *culminating* in jhana. Whatever degree of concentration you have can be considered Right Concentration, as long as it is accompanied by Right Understanding, Right Intention, and the other elements of the Eightfold Path. Holding concentration with this attitude can support you in staying easeful and relaxed, helping you avoid overstriving or struggle even as you remain conscientious and committed in your meditation.

Chapter 6

DEEPENING CONCENTRATION

With growing concentration and heightened mindfulness, meditation opens in whole new directions as our efforts bear deepening fruit. Supported by the steady presence you have been cultivating, what had been difficult or a struggle now comes almost effortlessly. Where you may have been plagued by hindrances or strove just to stay present for a few breaths, you are now opening to a degree of ease and clarity inaccessible in the beginning.

This can be an inspiring time, encouraging and sustaining your continued practice. As peace, calm presence, openhearted kindness, and all the benefits you have been receiving on the meditation cushion are carried through into the rest of your life, you may feel a growing sense of gratitude and a deeper motivation to explore where this journey of self-discovery might lead.

This is also a time to notice if you fall into craving or clinging. Just as we can easily get caught up in ordinary life, we can become enthralled with the progression of meditation. We do not want to turn what is wholesome and meant to help us come to an end of suffering into a source of clinging. If you find yourself pushing to make the concentration better or stronger or more blissful, try to relax and let go into whatever is happening, whether it is a time of discomfort or ease. Stay with the simple mindfulness of breathing practice, however the process continues to reveal itself. Let the power of the concentration you have developed support an even deeper, more sustained connection with your breath.

By now you are well acquainted with meditation's challenges and rewards. Bring the skills in mindfulness you have been developing to meet and work with all the inevitable ups and downs. Notice what is happening and how you are relating to the unfolding process. The same equanimity you employed to prevent you from falling into aversion with hindrances will help you avoid the trap of craving for the pleasure of concentration.

Ways of Unfolding

Deepening practice can develop in a variety of ways. As your ability to remain undistracted grows, the experiences associated with concentration can become much stronger and more compelling, and will tend to fill more and more of your consciousness. Concentration and the physical sensations of breathing may begin to mix, merge, or interact in a variety of ways.

Sometimes the physical breath will expand out naturally and be experienced through the entire abdomen, torso, shoulders, or head. Or awareness can shift from the gross physical sensations of the breath to subtler inner sensations, which can be experienced as patterns of energy in the body.

We discussed previously how sometimes the sensations of breathing can be more prominent than the experiences of concentration, and other times the concentration can become stronger in your awareness than the breath. This dynamic can also shift so you feel the concentration and the breath merging until they become one blended experience. No longer feeling the physical sensations of breathing as being separate from the experiences of concentration, you now find that the object of your attention is transformed into a new experience, breath and concentration unified into what we can call the *samadhi-breath*. You might experience the samadhi-breath as the breath blended with light, energy, pleasure, stillness, sound, or any of the experiences we have been talking about. Or, rather than merging just with the breath, samadhi also can expand beyond the breath to fill your whole body.

If subtle breath energy, or any other samadhi experience, suffuses throughout your body, let the process happen. Perhaps you will still be able to individually discern the breath and the concentration, or the concentration suffused throughout the body, but the sense of them merged into one will be stronger. If any of these phenomena happen, let the feeling of breath expanded through the body or the blended experience become the new object of your meditation practice. Stay with the new blended or expanded experience, just as you have been working with the breath from the beginning.

The merging of samadhi and breath, or the expanding of breath to fill the whole body, may happen naturally; or you may choose to direct your attention to move in these directions, if you feel yourself becoming less connected with the sense of your body. In our discussion of Right Concentration we said there are two main directions in which concentration can head: toward inclusive concentration or exclusive concentration. For some of us, the experience of concentration will naturally expand to suffuse the body. If samadhi has pervaded your entire body, you are naturally heading in the direction of inclusive, embodied unification of mind, and you do not have to do anything except let the process unfold on its own. Do not try to get back to the breath. Continue mindfully connecting with the whole body. The breath will have done its job.

Meditation can also progress in the opposite direction. Rather than feeling embodied, you can become increasingly engrossed in the concentration experiences themselves. If these experiences become quite strong and compelling, you may feel drawn into them. You may want to leave any feeling of your body behind and go into these experiences—we call it becoming absorbed in them—ever more deeply. Becoming less connected with and aware of the body, you are becoming more engaged with and absorbed in the purely mental experience of the pleasure, the light or the bliss.

You are headed toward a one-pointed, disembodied, exclusive concentration. If you were to follow that and let the bliss fill more and more of your awareness, you would eventually lose awareness of your body altogether and only the experience of light or bliss would remain.

Steering Toward Inclusive Concentration

Since we are aiming for inclusive, embodied samadhi, as the concentration becomes stronger, notice in which direction you are inclining. Check in once or twice during a sitting period to see if you have a sense of being connected with your body or not. For many people there is neither a strong, obvious pull into the concentration and away from the body, nor a strong sense of concentration being embodied. In this case simply stay with the mindful breathing or with the blended samadhi-breath, however you experience it. You are entering a subtle realm, where the distinction between embodied and disembodied concentration may not be easily discernible.

There may not be much experience in your body to connect with because everything may be so quiet and still, but you will still have some sense of knowing there is a body, or that you are losing that awareness. The normal sense of solidity can dissolve as you begin to perceive your body as being composed of energy, vibration, or light. Everything can become so tranquil and still that, while you are still connected with and have a sense of the body, there is not much happening to experience.

You may need to purposefully turn away from exclusive concentration and steer yourself in the direction of inclusive samadhi. If the sensations of breath take on a body of their own or begin to feel disconnected, you are heading into a purely mental experience. That is the time to incline your mind or coax it back and suffuse your awareness throughout the body. If meditation is unfolding this way for you, once the experiences of concentration become quite compelling, rather than having all your attention absorbed or pulled into them, do precisely the opposite—pull them into and suffuse them throughout your body.

You can do that by turning your attention back to your body. Put your awareness on your body, connecting with it wherever and in whatever way you experience it. Because the power of your concentrated mind is so strong, simply by placing your awareness on your body, consciously turning your attention to it, the concentration will turn in to the body with you and will pervade throughout your body on its own.

You do not want to do this too early in the process. You will know when the time is right by paying attention to what happens. You will know if it is too early; if you were not that concentrated, in turning your attention away from the samadhi or the samadhi-breath and toward awareness of your body, you will tend to lift out of the concentration. You will clearly see that your mind is less settled.

And you will know if you waited too long because you will have become fully absorbed into the mental samadhi experience and all awareness of your body will have vanished. Do not worry if this happens. You will have gained experience for the next time to better know when to turn back to your body before the connection is severed. You will know if you turned your attention back at the right time because the experiences of bliss, energy, light, or peace will go into your body and fill it, and it will continue opening in that direction on its own as you settle further in concentration.

Deepening of Letting Go

Bring however much effort is needed to your meditation but no more; use the lightest touch of attention necessary for staying present and connected. Balance making effort with letting go, so that the building momentum takes over and does more of the work for you. Let the concentration itself carry you further into the practice. You may have a feeling of wanting to try harder and push with the mind. This is not a physical sense of pushing; it is increasing your effort beyond simply connecting with and sustaining your attention on the meditation object—going beyond that to a mental feeling of working harder to press your attention and immerse awareness even more fully into the meditation object. If you try pressing with your awareness, pay attention to whether it causes agitation or helps you deepen.

At some point you will have to let go of pushing. It is too much mental doing and ultimately hinders the subtler stages of letting go required to drop into jhana. We sometimes have a tendency to keep increasing effort as concentration strengthens, but this can be counterproductive. The deeper stages of samadhi are stages of letting go, not stages of more doing. Let the momentum take over and carry you. This is the doorway into jhana.

Chapter 7

Strong Energies and Challenging Experiences

I f you meditate you are going to get more concentrated, and with concentration come both opportunities and challenges. Deepening concentration brings new possibilities for growth, but we need to acknowledge and be respectful of the very real and powerful energies, emotions, memories, and somatic experiences that can accompany the growing steadiness and clarity.

We cannot fully know all that might arise in our practice, so we need to have the skills and tools to work with anything that happens. We need to learn to navigate the terrain, familiarizing ourselves with the landscape of consciousness with appreciation for both its potential and pitfalls, and we need to bring an open, receptive attitude and a willingness to stay present with what is happening for us. With guidance and experience we develop resources and skills to meet anything we encounter—listening carefully, paying attention, and acknowledging our limitations and knowing when and how to back off.

The progression of deepening samadhi is highly individual. For some people meditation unfolds in a way that is very smooth and calm from beginning practice through the subtlest stages of jhana, without a lot of strong energetic experiences. For others the progression of meditation can be quite powerful and dramatic.

Working with the Pleasure

The pleasure of concentration helps loosen our mundane attachments and the pull of ordinary sense pleasures. As the pleasure of concentration strengthens, sensual desires begin to lose their grip on us. Because the contentment of a quiet mind is more satisfying than ordinary worldly enjoyments, the power and allure of worldly pleasures start to diminish, without us having to do much to make it happen.

But because the pleasure of concentration is so compelling, we may begin meditating just in order to have more. This is why some teachers invalidate these experiences or would have us avoid them, concerned that they will serve only to increase craving. But just as we should not make too much of them, neither should we deny the pleasure and profundity such experiences offer.

We should not be afraid of the pleasure of concentration; the pleasure serves an important function in furthering the deepening process. The Buddha called jhana the pleasure associated with renunciation, seclusion, peace, and enlightenment. He said we should seek out and develop this kind of pleasure, that it should not be avoided or feared.

Deepening concentration offers us challenges and opportunities. When we touch it we are happy; it feels right and good. The art and skill of meditation rests in understanding how to employ this pleasure as an aid for immersing ourselves more fully, more deeply into the meditation without turning what is a wholesome, skillful, and powerful aid on the path to enlightenment into a source of craving. Chasing after or clinging to some experience is a sure way to increase your suffering and to cut yourself off from the very meditative states you seek to develop.

This is the time to recollect and connect with your intentions, enlisting all the supports you have been developing. If we do not know what our intentions are, our actions are liable to be dictated by our feelings and moods, especially when the power and energy of a situation is strong. Let your wholesome intention act as a touchstone. Make it the standard by which you make decisions, instead of following after the moment's appeal.

The natural tendency to be drawn toward pleasant experiences is deeply ingrained in all of us. But even during the most intense times, when the pleasures enthrall us, we can avoid becoming seduced by them. Gather all the mindfulness and clarity of awareness you are able to access, and rest in the protection of your wholesome intention.

When we are clear about our intention, fascinating experiences do not delude or deceive us. We remember that our intention is the liberation pointed to by the Buddha, not to collect one more exciting experience that is only going to come and go like all the others before it.

You never have to worry about being too concentrated as long as that concentration is Right Concentration. Remember that samadhi, the term we translate as "concentration," actually means "undistracted." You can never be too undistracted as long as you have an inclusive awareness along with mindfulness and equanimity to the extent necessary for meeting whatever degree of concentration there is.

Balancing Energy

While you cannot be too concentrated, you can have the wrong kind of concentration or an unbalanced concentration. Energy, or any of the experiences we are talking about that are associated with concentration, can be too strong for us or of a quality that we are not able to handle.

After discussing some of the ways unbalanced concentration can manifest, we will examine various approaches for working with them. Anything that can arise in meditation can be worked with. With proper tools you will learn to navigate all of meditation's ups and downs, meeting whatever happens with confidence and clarity.

Strong energies can course through the body, and can be associated with pleasure, bliss, or light, or they can be highly unpleasant or agitating. Some meditators may experience loud inner sounds. These experiences can be agreeable and satisfying, or they may become unpleasant or too much for us to handle. These energies can remain localized in one place, or they can move around or permeate the entire body. They can remain at the same intensity, weaken, or grow, and their location and strength can fluctuate in regular cycles or appear sporadically. All of this is dependent upon our individual dispositions, the sensitivities of our nervous systems, and our psychosomatic conditioned patterns.

Concentration tends to suppress the hindrances, gladdening our hearts and calming our minds. Unpleasant or challenging thoughts and feelings tend not to come up when our minds are settled. But being concentrated can also have the opposite effect. Concentration tends to permeate and pervade whatever experience is most prominent, so difficult states of mind may become magnified rather than suppressed.

As your experiences of concentration become stronger and your mind becomes increasingly focused, the concentration tends to enhance those experiences. A memory or story can become blown up and because your perception has been altered you may not be able to tell. The exaggerated version becomes your reality and you believe it.

A student once told me of a time on a meditation retreat when she went looking for something to eat in the community refrigerator, a place where extra food—fruit, bread, cheese, and nut butters—was made available for anyone who got hungry between meals. Just as she opened the refrigerator she noticed a disapproving look from one of the retreat center staff who happened to walk past.

She had gotten into a very quiet, concentrated place and from that one glance tumbled into a story that she had done something terrible, had somehow broken the rules by being in that refrigerator, that she was being judged for eating between meals when she should be meditating and, finally, that she was going to be kicked out of the retreat. Nothing came of it and at the end of the retreat she asked the person about it. That staff person had no recollection of the incident. An incidental glance, of no consequence but perceived in a certain way, got interpreted and ascribed with a world of meaning.

We tend not to notice when our minds go into this kind of proliferation. We can just believe the stories we are making up, imagining the worst possible reasons or motives and the most terrible outcomes, spinning out more stories from the stories, without recognizing the process that is going on. We create entire realities and proceed to live in those worlds as if they were real.

You can be resting peacefully in meditation when some old, forgotten memory suddenly pops into your mind. Maybe you recall something you did that caused harm to others or pain for yourself and you are filled with regret, guilt, or shame. And because you are so concentrated, that hurt becomes magnified and fills your consciousness, and you are completely back reliving that old experience, submerged in the old feelings.

Old traumas can be activated in concentrated states, triggering upsetting memories of physical injury or emotional, psychological, or sexual abuse. Or patterns of fear, worry, self-judgment, or any parts of your life you deal with regularly can come roaring up, seemingly stronger than ever. Desire or longing in some part of your life, something you struggle with daily, can feel like it is going to overwhelm you.

Entering Unfamiliar Territory

We may enter new territory of consciousness where familiar reference points start to disappear. For many people this never happens, but for some, deepening concentration can open to altered experiences in which their normal sense of reality begins to break down.

We may perceive our body as being composed of energy, vibration, or light, and the border between our inner and outer world may become less obvious. It can be disconcerting to feel the solidity and boundary we are used to experiencing begin to melt. You might sense your body grown to many times normal, perhaps feeling as if it fills the entire room. The feeling can be so real that you are convinced you have actually physically expanded, and you have to open your eyes to see that your body is actually normal size.

Through the power of our concentrated mind we may open to perceptions of impermanence where our body and the external world, everything that had seemed solid and stable, now appears to be in constant flux. You may find yourself on a knife-edge between past and future as the present moment dissolves right out from under you. We can become frightened if our perception of impermanence gets ahead of our equanimity.

If we find ourselves in terrain with which we are unfamiliar, we may become disoriented. If anything happens that we are unaccustomed to, we may feel shaky or fearful. Though these occurrences do not happen for everyone, any of the experiences associated with concentration can become strong and we need some skillful means for working with them when they do.

Two Main Approaches

For all of these reasons, we need to be respectful of the potential for anything to happen, and we need to develop our capacity for dealing with whatever might arise.

There are two main approaches for dealing with any strong or unfamiliar conditions we may encounter in meditation. We can bring down the intensity of the situation or we can bring up and strengthen our mindfulness, equanimity, and ability to be present with those experiences. Knowing which approach to take, when to turn toward a situation and when to change our circumstances or move away, is an art—an art that we can develop with experience.

Bringing Up Ability to Be With Strong Experiences

When the situation is within our capability but we just do not like what is happening, we have to find a way to wait for it to subside on its own. We need confidence in our ability to learn how to be with things, developing patience and a capacity to hang in there through the turbulent times.

Cultivating self-reliance may require some trial and error, but over time and with experience we know we can trust ourselves. We know we do not have to believe our stories, fears, perceptions, or moods, because we recognize that these things come and go. We have seen over and over that every experience we have ever had has passed. And we know the same is true for every experience we are ever going to have. Because we have seen that these things come and go, we know how to be with them all and we know we will emerge from them in time.

One meditator, some days into an intensive retreat, reported having a song suddenly pop into his mind. The song kept looping, repeating over and over, and this went on for two days. He pushed against it, struggling to turn it off, but he found that pushing only fed it, giving it energy. After half a day he was crying for mercy and finally he gave up, let go, and just waited. After two days it disappeared on its own.

Sometimes, all we need is simply to identify what is happening, acknowledging if the energy feels strong or edgy, or if it feels like too much. Just by recognizing our experience and how we are relating with what is happening, we are able to summon the resources needed to meet these challenging forces, strengthening mindfulness and resting in the undistracted knowing while the process unfolds.

If mindfulness is well established and stability is firm, it does not matter how powerful the samadhi experience is because we are steady, we are undistracted, and we can take refuge in the mindfulness itself. Mindfulness and equanimity help create the container to hold samadhi experiences. When there is too little of either, we are liable to be pulled out of a balanced presence; but these experiences do not bother us if we can meet them with equanimity and clear awareness. We do not have to do anything with them. When mindfulness is clear and balance is strong, we can perceive that whatever happens is just another experience that arises and passes away, without grasping at it or pushing it away.

Try bringing in a quality of observing, rather than becoming caught up, lost, or identified with the experience. You can notice that there is awareness or mindfulness and that you can relax back into and rest in the pure knowing of the experience. You are still having the experience but you are aware of being aware. You know that you know. And that can often be a very strong stabilizing force to help work with what is happening.

Resting in the knowing does not mean being a disconnected or detached witness, untouched by what is happening. You are fully in the experience, but in a way that is disentangled and unfettered. Such an untroubled and unburdened abiding can act as the safe container for letting go. You can be more deeply present without agitation and can more fully know, not as a concept but as directly experienced, that this mental, physical, or emotional phenomenon is just another part of the stream of consciousness that arises and passes away due to its own causes and conditions.

Taking refuge in the knowing and in the letting go, we gain access to a clear, quiet strength and fearlessness, enabling us to be present and to let go even more fully. We can be fearless because we know we are protected, no matter what happens. We have established a secure footing for venturing forth.

Sometimes we are able to be present with whatever is happening, but we are afraid of what might happen next. For many people fear is highly unpleasant. Noticing that fear is present and how unpleasant it is may be just enough support for us to stay with the experience more fully.

I have had very powerful experiences arise while meditating, followed by fear that those experiences were going to keep intensifying. But then I would remember to drop back and rest in awareness as a refuge. From that place all the experiences could arise and pass away and whatever happened was not a problem.

Bringing Down Intensity

Along with broadening skills for how to be present with something, we must learn how and when to interrupt the process. If you have tried working with the meditation and it still feels like too much, you may need a break. We need to be respectful of samadhi's power and of our boundaries and capabilities. Being honest about what is happening includes being honest about our ability to relate to what is happening.

Use your best judgment on how to proceed and try not to disparage yourself as a bad meditator, thinking that you should stay with an experience when in reality dealing with it is beyond your capacity. If your mindful presence or equanimity is not sufficient to meet the concentration, find a way to limit or stop the process. If you are not able to be clear, mindful, steady, and present, you need to acknowledge that fact. You may need to bring down the intensity, smooth the rough edges, or pull out of the meditation entirely.

From the beginning days of your meditation you have been cultivating the ability to direct your awareness by returning over and over to your breathing. Now, use the skills you have developed to redirect your attention away from the intensity and toward something nurturing and sustaining.

Try putting your attention to some place in your body that feels steady. Feel your body sitting in the chair or your bottom or legs pressing on the cushion or bench wherever you are sitting. Feel your arms and legs. Put your attention anywhere you can in your body to help yourself feel more embodied and grounded. If the energy is strong, let it flow out your hands and feet and drain into the ground. Take some calming breaths, breathing in a sense of peace and calm and breathing out the energy. Or try opening your eyes and looking around to reconnect and get back into the normal world. Perhaps get up and walk around, go outside, or engage in mundane activities, feeling your feet or legs as you move. Try anything like this you can do to be more grounded and get back to your ordinary, everyday reality.

And then, when you are ready, if you are ready, you can come back, either in this session or another—back into the practice. In this way we learn with experience when it is time to bring the energy and intensity down, when it is time to back off and come out of the meditation, and when to stay with it by strengthening the presence of mind and equanimity, the pure mindfulness that enables us to rest more fully with whatever is happening.

We want to be respectful and not push ourselves into anything. Sometimes you touch on something and then you pull back. But then you touch it again and pull back over and over until you gain some familiarity, letting mindfulness be your refuge, so that even if something is completely unfamiliar and you do not know what is happening, you can rest at peace in mindful presence.

Chapter 8

JHANA: THE CULMINATION OF CONCENTRATION

After embarking on his spiritual quest, leaving home, family, and the comfortable, secure life he had known, Siddhartha Gotama, the Buddha-to-be, spent the next six years engaged in a variety of stringent spiritual practices. You will sometimes see statues and images of a skeletal Buddha, representing the ascetic Gotama, emaciated through years of austerity and self-denial. He almost died before realizing that ascetic practices and self-mortification were dead ends that did not lead to liberation from the human condition.

As he had this realization he remembered a time from his childhood, sitting in the shade of a rose-apple tree watching his father plowing a field, when he spontaneously entered a deep state of samadhi, the first jhana. He was feeling happy, relaxed and at ease in the beauty of that orchard, and naturally fell into this blissful state of peace and calm.

And now, his body wasted and near death, he considered whether that same state of clarity and ease could be the way forward. Realizing that jhana was where the path to enlightenment lay and that it would be hard to attain that state in such an emaciated condition, he began to eat, caring for his body and regaining strength. He then turned his attention in a new direction, to the cultivation of Right Samadhi—tranquility and insight yoked evenly together in jhana.

It is hard to overstate the significance of jhana in the Buddha's path of meditation. Over and over the Buddha emphasized its importance. He practiced jhana on the night of his enlightenment, he taught jhana to his students, and after his enlightenment he would sometimes withdraw his mind in jhana. He had developed the ability, the mastery, to access these absorption states whenever he chose.

 A mind well concentrated is purified, bright, unblemished, rid of imperfection, flexible, steady, and attained to imperturbability. Such a mind has a penetrative power far surpassing ordinary awareness; it can perceive reality on whole new levels and, when turned toward awakening and liberation, can see the subtle places of suffering and the ways we can truly rest in the stream of nonclinging.

What Is Jhana?

Jhana is dramatically different from the ordinary daily consciousness in which most of us spend our lives. For many, jhana seems exotic and far away from any experience they can relate to or imagine attaining. But as your practice matures, you come to know the extent to which meditative consciousness can evolve. If you have ever sat an intensive meditation retreat, you see how far your practice can develop in just a few days. Jhana is not only for ascetics living in caves. Real meditators just like you have realized the benefits jhana has to offer.

Recall that as meditation progresses, the unfolding of undistractedness can diverge, heading either toward increasing disconnection from or toward enhanced awareness of your body and mind. Jhana is the culmination of samadhi that is connected. Jhana is a state of deep calm, undistracted clarity, and enhanced connection with and profound insight into the nature of the body and the mind.

Because in jhana your mind is so highly attuned and sensitive, you are opening to perceptions on much more refined levels. You may perceive your body as being made of energy vibrations or light. You become effortlessly aware of subtle thoughts or impulses. At this stage your body and mind may be calmed to such a high degree there is not a lot of mental and physical activity to experience, but you do not need much to be aware of since the mind is so sensitive and attuned. Heightened awareness of and connection with the body is both an essential characteristic of jhana and, as we shall see, a way leading to it.

Defining Jhana

Four jhanas are described in the Buddhist texts, comprising progressively subtler stages of increasing calm, clarity, and peace. The four jhanas are not actually four separate discrete states; each is a marker along a continuum. While some of the attributes of the first jhana drop away as you progress through the stages, others are retained, though they may become smoother and subtler from one jhana to the next.

To understand the nature of jhana and how to access and progress through the stages, we will begin by exploring the first jhana. Once we understand the first jhana, what the experience of it is like and how to attain it, we will examine aspects of jhana in general. Then we will come back to the four jhanas in sequence, proceeding from the first jhana through the even subtler stages of concentration: the second, third, and fourth jhanas.

The first jhana is defined by this formula:

> Quite secluded from sensual pleasures, secluded from unwholesome states, one enters and abides in the first jhana [which is characterized by] rapture and pleasure born of seclusion, and accompanied by thought and examination.

"Secluded from sensual pleasures" means having established supportive conditions for entering the deeper stages of samadhi. We can meditate in any surroundings, but our minds will not settle down easily if we are flooded with a constant stream of sense inputs. To cultivate internal seclusion we must create the proper environment for it, and promote wholesome qualities of our hearts and minds. We need to find a time and place best suited to meditation within the constraints of our life circumstances. All the qualities we have been cultivating throughout the course of our meditation—living ethically in accordance with the precepts, balanced effort, ease and relaxation, and a sense of self-compassion—now come to fruition, arriving to meet us as supporting allies.

Through our many encounters with difficulties in meditation we have learned to set aside sensual desire and craving for pleasure, aversion toward difficult and unpleasant experiences, restlessness, sloth and torpor, and doubt. As we near jhana our mind has become even more quiet and calm. This is called "secluded from unwholesome states" because as we approach jhana our mind is so still that the hindrances cannot arise.

Factors of the First Jhana

The four qualities listed in the definition of the first jhana—rapture, pleasure, thought, and examination—along with a fifth factor identified elsewhere in the source texts, unification of mind, comprise the standard list known as the five jhana factors. All five of these factors are present in the first jhana.

The Pali term *piti*, which is translated here as "rapture," is also translated as "bliss" or "joy." It refers to all the various experiences of samadhi we have been discussing throughout this book, which can appear as bliss or pleasant experiences of energy, light, or sound. As we have emphasized, how rapture manifests itself is highly individual. *Sukha*, translated here as "pleasure," and sometimes as "happiness," refers to these same experiences when they have smoothed out and subside in intensity. Some people have very dramatic experiences of rapture in the first jhana, while for others it is very smooth, even, and calm. The happiness or pleasure of jhana can be thick like honey or, as the jhana progresses, thin out to be very light and sweet.

"Thought and examination" does not refer to thinking in the ordinary sense that we are used to in everyday life. In the first jhana some thoughts can arise, but they are greatly diminished—they are quiet and subtle, and are seen and known as they arise. We are never lost in or identified with them. Thought and examination here involve unifying the whole mind—bringing all its capacities, including its thinking capacity, together in undistracted awareness. They include directing and sustaining attention to the meditation object. This kind of mental activity is self-sustaining and self-directing, like a gentle guiding or inclining of the mind. In any of the jhanas, though the undistractedness of mind is unshakeable, a slight amount of directing of attention can happen. As factors of jhana, "thought and examination" entail directing this attention to the meditation object so that the mind can be applied to and sustained on that object.

Using stock phrases, as is common in the Pali texts, the jhana definitions are often accompanied by beautiful similes that expand upon and illuminate the meaning. The similes not only complement the description in the definitions, they also explain the way to realize jhana and how to advance through the successive stages.

The simile for the first jhana is:

He makes the rapture and pleasure born of seclusion drench, steep, fill, and pervade this body, so that there is no part of his whole body unpervaded by the rapture and pleasure born of seclusion. Just as a skilled bath man or a bath man's apprentice heaps bath powder in a metal basin and, sprinkling it gradually with water, kneads it till the moisture wets his ball of bath powder, soaks it and pervades it inside and out, yet the ball itself does not ooze; so too, a *bhikkhu* [monk] makes the rapture and pleasure born of seclusion drench, steep, fill, and pervade this body, so that there is no part of his whole body unpervaded by the rapture and pleasure born of seclusion.

In the first jhana awareness is deeply immersed in and suffused throughout the body, as clearly expressed in the simile. But though you are profoundly connected and intimate with the body, the experience of the body is altered from what is accessible through our ordinary sense perceptions. The sense of solidity may give way to subtler sensations of vibration or a sense of the body dissolving away.

The Experience of Jhana

We have seen that the quality and intensity of deepening concentration can manifest in a variety of ways, differing greatly from one person to another. You might experience the jhana factors rapture and pleasure as blissful bodily sensations of energy, vibration, light, or sound. The feelings can be very powerful, pouring over you like a waterfall, or may only be very soft and light.

Meditators sometimes judge their progress solely in terms of the presence of the jhana factors and the absence of the five hindrances. Because jhana is defined by a standard formula, they may believe there are certain milestones to be met, well defined and common for everyone along this path. They may think they are in jhana if rapture and pleasure are strong.

It is a mistake to see the jhana factors as the sole criteria for judging whether or not you have attained the first jhana. Even in the beginning stages of meditation, when concentration is just beginning to blossom, you can feel pleasure. Your mind can be more unified and less distracted. As samadhi strengthens, the jhana factors may become more pronounced, but even in jhana how the factors present themselves is highly individual. We cannot say jhana is marked for everyone by any particular expression of rapture and pleasure. If you have a preconceived idea of what kind of or how much rapture or pleasure you are supposed to have, you may find yourself striving for that. Remember that the stages of jhana are stages of letting go, not of gaining. If you find yourself comparing and judging, try to let it go. You will suffer less and progress faster.

Three Essential Characteristics of Jhana

Jhana is a distinctive state marked by three universal qualities. These three qualities are hallmarks of all four stages of jhana. For anyone in jhana the mind is utterly undistracted and incapable of wandering even for a moment, it is extraordinarily lucid and clear, and the meditation proceeds entirely on its own, with no sense that you are doing anything to sustain it. Whenever these three aspects are present, regardless of the experiences accompanying them, jhana has been reached. If these are not all present and fully developed you cannot call the meditative state jhana.

Unification of Mind

The first quality of jhana is sustained, unbroken mindfulness. An untrained mind tends to be easily distracted, never really settled, and quick to jump from one thing to another. It is striking, and a big relief, when our mind first begins to quiet down in the early development of concentration. Once concentration is very strong, our minds may not wander much—perhaps only for a moment or so, in the deeper stages, before we come back. Perhaps the mind does not wander at all and there is only an impulse for the mind to start to drift or a slight agitation or instability within awareness. Once you are in jhana all of that movement is gone. The mind cannot wander or even have an impulse to wander at all as long as you are in that meditative state.

As autumn gives way to winter, snow can turn into a slushy mixture of water and ice, thicker than liquid, before finally freezing completely. The icy water is undoubtedly freezing, but there is no mistaking slush for solid ice. If your mind can move even a slight amount, you are not in jhana. You may be close, but once in jhana your mind will be immovable in sustained undistractedness.

Though your mind in jhana cannot move from unbroken mindfulness, there remains a part of your mind that *can* move, to incline your attention in particular directions. This is a very subtle movement. We will explore this in detail later in this chapter and in the next.

Heightened Clarity

The second quality universal to everyone in jhana is increased clarity of mind. Compared to ordinary states of mind, we can see how much more aware we naturally are of subtle aspects of experience when concentration is very strong. Once you have entered jhana, that clarity of awareness is heightened to a whole new level that was previously inaccessible.

You may notice the genesis of thoughts (in the first jhana— thoughts do not arise in the other jhanas), the first impulse for them appearing even before breaking to the surface of consciousness. In jhana your body and mind are tranquilized so that there may not be a lot to experience beyond the jhana factors themselves. But your perception is so clear and bright that you are keenly attuned to whatever does arise. It is like bringing a light to a darkened room. Where you previously could only make out shadows or vague forms, now you see everything in sharp detail.

Self-Sustaining

The third central jhana quality is a sense of self-sustaining. Not only is the mindfulness unbroken, the mind unwavering, but the process of meditation is unfolding on its own without you doing anything to make it happen or keep it going. As concentration builds, meditation starts to feel more effortless. Even in the early stages, meditation feels easier when you are settled and clear compared to the times when your mind is hazy and you cannot focus. The momentum of the concentration carries you and there is not so much you have to do to keep the practice going. You are still putting in some amount of effort, you still incline your mind to connect with objects of meditation, but with a lighter and lighter touch. Perhaps there is only a slight turning of your attention to connect with your breathing.

In jhana, the sense of having to do anything to maintain the meditation, even on the subtlest levels, is gone. As long as you are in jhana the meditation is completely effortless and self-sustaining.

These three aspects of jhana—the unbroken awareness, the heightened clarity, and the self-sustaining or effortlessness—are common hallmarks for everyone. Along with these there may be other experiences, such as the jhana factors, which can vary greatly from one person to another. Some people may not experience much else besides the sustained clarity and a sense of calm and stillness. For others jhana can be accompanied by very powerful lights, energies, or other blissful experiences.

As you get close to jhana it is important to distinguish between the experiences of concentration—the bliss, light, or energy—and the undistracted clarity itself. Deepening stages of samadhi and jhana are not stages of gaining new experiences, but stages of letting go. Some people become caught up in or fascinated with these dramatic experiences. But ultimately they all drop away, especially when you get to the third and fourth jhanas, leaving only the clear, bright mind. Be aware of how the jhana factors are arising for you, but mostly stay attuned and interested in the three main qualities that will help you attain and then advance through the progressive, subtler stages of jhana.

How to Attain Jhana

Meditators will sometimes wonder: *Is this jhana?* You can be sitting right on the doorstep and not know. You cannot know how close you are until you have made the transition and see what it looks like on the other side. Once you enter jhana, there is no longer any doubt. Once you cross the threshold, you access a degree of steadiness and self-continuation that is striking, a qualitative shift to an entirely new level of clarity, steadiness, and self-sustained presence.

Maturing of Right Effort

Sensing they are close to jhana but unable to take hold of it, people can sometimes become more frustrated or impatient. Agitation can feed back onto itself, pulling you out of concentration and causing even more aggravation as any remnants of clarity and calm melt away.

Nonclinging is the fruit of dharma practice, but is also the way forward itself. By remembering to meet your meditation with an experimental attitude, a willingness to stay present and learn what works and what does not, you have gained wisdom and skill. From all the times you kept sitting through worry, frustration, or pain you have developed the capacity for patience. Kindness for ourselves, discernment, and mindfulness are all essential for attaining jhana. But these qualities are not merely tools to aid us in our journey. The wholesome qualities we have been developing to reach jhana are their own reward; they are themselves the fruit of our practice. Embracing an attitude of the path as the goal supports us to relax and be at ease, makes the qualities of a liberated mind come alive for us now, and offers the fastest way toward realizing jhana.

If you have never played the piano, you would not expect to have any skill at it. But by just beginning, though you have no ability whatsoever, your playing will improve. The same is true in meditation. By applying yourself, doing the best you can, you move from tenuous first steps to competence and skill. Reflect on and acknowledge what you have learned. You have put in time and energy, sitting when you were inspired and carrying on when you didn't want to, through all the ups and downs, and you are learning how to do it.

Entering the First Jhana

Entering jhana happens on its own. You cannot make it happen. The stages of jhana are not progressive stages of doing or gaining; they are deepening levels of letting go and simplifying the mind. We cannot force the blossoming of jhana any more than we can force a flower to open—the very act of trying is too much mental activity for the mind to settle down completely. But while we cannot force a flower to open, we can provide everything the flower needs to blossom. Similarly, there are things we can do to facilitate the process of jhana, and to create the conditions necessary for the mind to drop into jhana when it is ready.

Stay aware of how much effort you are making and in what directions your effort is aimed. Like the Buddha, we can learn this skill if we apply ourselves with patience. The key to doing this is not complicated. Just carry on with the simple form of connecting with your body breathing and let the process continue to unfold.

Use the breath as skillful means in support of letting go. Do not try to press or force yourself to attain jhana, or any other state of meditation. Pushing is counterproductive because it is too much doing, too much activity, when what we want is for the mind to settle, not do. Try to let go of your struggles and let go of clinging to pleasure. Simply attend wisely to whatever is happening moment by moment. Practicing in this way aims us toward jhana with a relaxed attitude that does not overstrive and allows the experiences of samadhi to develop organically.

You still have to make some amount of effort until you are in jhana, but it becomes an ever lighter touch until finally you have let go completely as the stream of samadhi carries you. You put in the work, make the effort toward building momentum, and then let the meditation's own power engage and take off.

You will know if you are striking the right balance between effort and letting go by paying attention to what happens as the momentum builds. If you are making too much effort, you may feel more agitation rather than more peace. Notice if you feel tense or tight or restless. Drop back and let go so that the momentum can take over. Shift from doing to feeling yourself being pulled in.

Similarly, notice what happens when you let go too soon. See if your mind wanders or moves more. If you let go too much before you are ready, you will feel yourself lifting out of the meditation. You will not be as concentrated. If this happens, bring back the effort and intention to direct the process more.

As the jhana factors strengthen, some teachers will advise letting go of the breath and shifting your attention solely to the pleasant aspect of your experience itself as your meditation object in order to bring you into jhana. However you are experiencing rapture and pleasure, connect with the pleasure itself as your meditation object. This may be helpful for some people and you can try it, but pay attention to what happens if you do.

Sometimes letting go into the pleasant feeling can help bring us further in, while for others staying with the breath works best. In any case, you cannot turn away from the breath and place your attention on pleasantness too soon or else you will lift out of the samadhi. By taking your attention away from the meditation object too early and putting it onto the pleasantness itself, you can feel yourself lifting out. You will not be as deeply concentrated. In this case bring your attention back to the samadhi-breath or the samadhi suffused throughout the body or whatever other meditation object you may have, letting go into that experience to take you deeper. You have to stay attuned and see what works best for you.

In previous chapters I discussed how, as concentration deepens, we can head in one of two directions, either more deeply immersed in body awareness or disconnected from consciousness of our body. Stay attuned to how the process is unfolding. As long as you have a sense of being connected with your body, though it may be quite subtle, continue practicing as you have been, either more narrowly focused in the area of the breath or opened up to the whole body. This will be your doorway into jhana.

If you feel like you are becoming disconnected from your body, then this is the time to intentionally turn your awareness into the body and, making as much effort as necessary but no more, suffuse the experiences of samadhi throughout your body. Let that be your doorway into jhana.

Recall the simile for the first jhana:

He makes the rapture and pleasure born of seclusion drench, steep, fill, and pervade this body, so that there is no part of his whole body unpervaded by the rapture and pleasure born of seclusion. Just as a skilled bath man or a bath man's apprentice heaps bath powder in a metal basin and, sprinkling it gradually with water, kneads it till the moisture wets his ball of bath powder, soaks it and pervades it inside and out, yet the ball itself does not ooze; so too, a bhikkhu [monk] makes the rapture and pleasure born of seclusion drench, steep, fill, and pervade this body, so that there is no part of his whole body unpervaded by the rapture and pleasure born of seclusion.

What is the bath man doing in this simile? He is making soap. He is combining water and bath powder, mixing and kneading them together until you no longer have two separate things. You have just the one thing, soap. Water and powder have unified into something new.

In precisely the same way, you make the rapture and pleasure, however you experience them, born of seclusion "drench, steep, fill, and pervade this body." You are bringing them into the body. This is a very clear, precise, and accurate description of what happens.

Rapture and pleasure suffused throughout the body is both the way into jhana and the nature of the state of the first jhana. You have been staying with the breath and now the instructions have changed. Notice there is no mention of the breath in the definition of jhana. The breath has done its job and now awareness has spread throughout the whole body. The meditator makes the rapture and pleasure drench, steep, fill, and pervade the body. You are consciously bringing it into the body if it is not happening on its own.

Entry into jhana is marked by an absorption into the rapture and pleasure suffused through the body. We are immersed in it. It permeates and soaks every part of us. For some, when the mind is ready it will drop into jhana of its own accord. Others may need to purposefully suffuse the samadhi experiences throughout the body, just as described in the simile. Stay with the process if it suffuses on its own, and guide it; suffuse it throughout the body if you need to.

Stabilizing Jhana

When you first touch jhana you may only stay in it for a short time before you are lifted right out. You may not know how you got in, how to stay in, or how to find your way back. Remember patience and try your best to let go of struggle or of trying to force the process. With time and experience you will find the way to jhana more consistently. As you take your time with each jhana, you will get to know it and learn how to move in and out of it.

As you begin to stabilize in jhana, you can hang out there and check out what it is like. How do you experience jhana? Is the rapture strong or light, edgy or smooth? Are there any thoughts? Notice the part of your mind that is unmoving and the part you can incline to investigate your experience. With only the barest, lightest touch, examine and get to know the surroundings. Do not be in a hurry. Without trying to get to the second jhana, spend some time noticing how things unfold.

Progressing Through the Jhanas

We move through the jhanas either by doing nothing and letting the process unfold on its own, or by doing something and engaging in the process of letting go.

For some, once the first jhana has been attained, progression happens on its own. If moving through the jhanas is going to happen on its own, you will feel yourself dropping down into deeper states. Whether the progression happens in a single sitting or over the course of months, you will not have to do anything and your mind will naturally settle, moving to the second jhana and beyond. Others may turn their minds toward simplifying and letting go to progress further. This can be a sense of letting go of the coarser experiences of the present jhana or of leaning into the subtler experiences of the next.

Directed Attention

The use of directed attention may be important for some people in order to progress through the jhanas, just as it was important throughout our meditation leading up to jhana. I have been emphasizing that, once in jhana, awareness is so stabilized there is not a sense of doing anything to keep the process going. The mind is undistracted and unmoving, and because it is absorbed in a steady awareness you cannot make mental effort in the ordinary sense. As you are carried with the unfolding progression, there is no sense of any activity on your part making it happen.

But even in the still places of meditative absorption and jhana there remains a part of the mind that can be inclined in certain directions. It sounds paradoxical that the mind is unmoving yet there is some part that *can* move, that our awareness can be directed somehow.

This is a subtle place in the meditation. A slight amount of knowing and directing of attention remains. The inclination of awareness is extremely delicate, but because your perception is so keen you do not need much other than a subtle awareness.

Second Jhana

With the stilling of thought and examination, he enters and abides in the second jhana [which is characterized by] rapture and pleasure born of concentration, and accompanied by inner composure and singleness of mind, without thought and examination.

The stars are always above us, but are obscured by the sun's brilliance by day. Only when the sun sets do the stars reveal themselves, coming to prominence in a powerful display against the night sky. The subtler features of jhana emerge as the coarser qualities fall away. This pattern will characterize progress through each of the jhanas.

The second jhana is more quiet and still than the first. The thought and examination of the first jhana have fallen away, rapture and pleasure remain, and other qualities, inner composure and singleness of mind, begin to emerge.

In the first jhana there can be some thoughts. With the stilling of thought and examination, the verbal process of thinking settles as you enter a wordless realm. The connecting and sustaining function of thought and examination is no longer necessary and drops away. Your awareness just *is* connected and sustained without the necessity of any mental function to sustain it. Inner composure and singleness of mind become more prominent as we find ourselves in a quieter, simpler place.

Listen to the simile for the second jhana:

> He makes the rapture and pleasure born of concentration
> drench, steep, fill, and pervade this body, so that there is no
> part of his whole body unpervaded by the rapture and plea-
> sure born of concentration. Just as though there were a lake
> whose waters welled up from below and it had no inflow
> from east, west, north or south and would not be replenished
> from time to time by showers of rain, then the cool fount of
> water welling up in the lake would make the cool water
> drench, steep, fill, and pervade the lake, so that there would
> be no part of the whole lake unpervaded by cool water; so
> too, a bhikkhu [monk] makes the rapture and pleasure born
> of concentration drench, steep, fill, and pervade this body, so
> that there is no part of his whole body unpervaded by the
> rapture and pleasure born of concentration.

Notice the shift from the first to the second jhana in the description of what happens. Just as in the first jhana, the rapture and pleasure drench, steep, fill, and pervade the body, but the image is
different. To get to the first jhana we are working and kneading, like
the bath man, putting in some amount of effort to suffuse the rapture
and pleasure throughout the body. The precise amount of effort
varies for each of us, depending on how the process unfolds on its
own, but there is some sense of directing the process.

Now, in the second jhana, the process of suffusing throughout
the body is still happening, but it is coming from a deeper place. It
feels a lot quieter. Instead of the external effort and energy of the
bath man, the infusion is welling up deep from within out of the
momentum and concentration of the first jhana.

Take some time and get to know what the second jhana is like.
Notice the wordless quality—you will not be thinking thoughts
about having no thoughts. This is a nonverbal knowing. Notice the
sense of inner composure and the undistracted singleness of mind.

Third Jhana

The third jhana is similar to the second, except it feels even smoother and more refined as rapture fades, leaving only pleasure:

> With the fading away of rapture, he abides in equanimity, mindful and clearly aware, feeling pleasure with the body, he enters and abides in the third jhana, of which the noble ones declare: "equanimous and mindful he abides in pleasure."

At some point the rapture we previously suffused throughout the body to access the first jhana begins to feel too energetic and coarse. The mind wants to settle further, and rapture gives way to a quieter pleasure in the body and happiness in the mind. For some, the rapture fades on its own as the third jhana begins to reveal itself. If this does not happen for you on its own, try inclining your mind, seeing if you can let go into the feeling of happiness or pleasure, something lighter than the rapture. If you are aware of your breathing, you can use it to help dissipate the rapture if that is strong.

Equanimity, mindfulness, and clear awareness are highlighted in the third jhana's definition. Our consciousness can be so filled by the rapture of the first and second jhanas that we may not notice the stability and clear awareness of our minds. As rapture subsides, mindfulness and equanimity come to prominence.

With attainment of the third jhana, the simile changes quite a bit:

> He makes the pleasure divested of rapture drench, steep, fill, and pervade this body, so that there is no part of his whole body unpervaded by the pleasure divested of rapture. Just as in a pond of blue or red or white lotuses, some lotuses that are born and grow in the water thrive, immersed in the water without ever rising out of it, and cool water drenches, steeps and pervades them from their tips to their roots, so there is no part of those lotuses unpervaded by the cool water, so too,

119

a bhikkhu [monk] makes the pleasure drench, steep and pervade the body.

There is no sense of doing here at all. There is more a sense of being. These lotuses are born, live their entire lives and die completely suffused in the water. They do not have to do anything to make it happen. In the third jhana the pleasure is suffused throughout your body without you doing anything to make it happen. It is a state of being, not of doing.

Fourth Jhana

Here is the definition of the fourth jhana:

With the abandoning of pleasure and pain, and with the previous disappearance of joy and grief, he enters and abides in the fourth jhana, [which has] neither-pain-nor-pleasure and purity of mindfulness and equanimity.

And here is the simile:

He sits pervading this body with a pure bright mind, so that there is no part of his whole body unpervaded by the pure bright mind. Just as though a man were sitting covered from head to foot with a white cloth, so that there would be no part of his whole body not covered by the white cloth; so, too, a bhikkhu [monk] sits pervading this body with a pure bright mind, so that there is no part of his whole body unpervaded by the pure bright mind.

With the abandoning of pleasure and pain you enter a state of great balance. There is no sense of doing, only a sense of being, and you just remain there. In the fourth jhana you are powerfully immersed in body awareness, a state of profound connection. With the settling out of rapture and pleasure, perceptions of your body become quite thin, and what remains is resting at peace in a bright, inclusive, equanimous awareness. Your experience of your body may be subtle; there may not be much to experience in the body at this point as the previous, coarser perceptions melt into vibration or light.

After Jhana

Once we are in any of the stages of jhana, our practice includes times of doing nothing and allowing the experiences and insights to reveal themselves, and times of inclining our minds toward investigation and inquiry. In the next chapter we will explore the various ways insight arises and its place on the path toward the ultimate goal of meditation: awakening and liberation through nonclinging.

As our familiarity with jhana grows, we learn to navigate the terrain, exploring the landscape of consciousness with increasing skill. We gain facility in moving about among the various levels and how to access and use pleasure to gladden our hearts and minds. As we touch the pleasure of concentration, the allure of worldly pleasure fades. A contented heart and mind are subtler, yet more satisfying, than anything that can be found through the ordinary senses. We see that we do not have to go looking outside ourselves. Worldly pleasure loses its attraction as we learn to let go into the more refined pleasure of concentration.

Jhana, like every other experience we can have, is not a reliable place to seek happiness. Though all of the jhanas are highly pleasant, even the purified realm of the fourth jhana contains the seeds of potential suffering. Each jhana has its own level of subtlety and satisfaction, but they all contain a degree of dissatisfaction. From the perspective of the earlier stages in meditation, the first jhana is appealing. From the perspective of the fourth jhana, it can feel rather crude.

By the time you have reached the fourth jhana your mind is keenly aware and you are able to perceive clinging on the subtlest levels. The jhanas are temporarily satisfying, but not ultimately satisfying; and clinging to jhana, or to any meditative state, plants the seeds of suffering.

And so jhana flows us toward awakening. Previously you realized that ordinary worldly pleasure is not fulfilling; now you realize that the pleasure of meditative states is not going to do it for you either. None of these states last, and once the energy of the meditation melts away, we are lifted out and back into the ordinary world. Now there is no turning back. This mind, which is purified, bright, unblemished, rid of imperfection, flexible, steady, and attained to imperturbability, now turns in a very profound way toward liberation.

Chapter 9

INSIGHT

I n the beginning instructions you were advised to find a posture where you could be as comfortable as possible. You could sit in a chair or even lie down, finding whatever best supported you to be relaxed, easeful, and alert. You did not have to make anything happen; all you had to do was be with your experience. By now you have seen how hard this simple notion, just to sit quietly and be present with yourself, can be.

The idea of nonclinging is simple, but one of the first insights we have is that this seemingly straightforward instruction, to be with ourselves, is hard to do. Letting go and nonclinging is easy when things are going your way, but you soon find all the ways you are unable to be present. You begin to uncover layer upon layer of reactive patterns pushing and pulling you in all directions. From all the times of sitting through knee pain or backache, staying with the practice when your mind would not cooperate or when you were visited by old memories or emotional pain, you learned to find moments of freedom in the midst of it all. And you discovered your edges, the places where you were not yet ready or able to let go of struggle, and learned how elusive the happiness of nonclinging can be.

Insight into anything means understanding its true nature. It is an intuitive knowing, direct perception of what is essentially true beyond mere intellectual understanding. To progress from a conceptual understanding of how dharma teachings and practice might help us to actualizing the dharma as a lived reality, we need help to realize the potential for quieting our minds and opening our hearts. We need to find the tools for meeting our self face to face. Through wise discernment we penetrate beneath surface appearances to recognize what is real and true about our world and ourselves.

Whenever you are suffering, it is a signal that you need to back up and look at what is keeping you from being present. And if you cannot be with that, you need to back up again, and keep doing so until you find what you *can* be present with. Insight is the discernment of your suffering, its cause, and a way to its end in order to more fully realize your capacity for letting go.

Insight is whatever perception or understanding sheds light on the places we create suffering and how to let that suffering go. Sometimes, when the light of awareness illuminates previously hidden corners of our psyche, old destructive patterns can fall away on their own. The grip of self-judgment, criticism, or doubt can loosen simply through mindful presence. Other times, mindful recognition is just the first step, a jumping off point for delving into something more deeply, thinking it through or feeling into it to untangle its knots.

How Insight Leads to Liberation

Just as we suffer in many ways and in many areas of our lives, so there are many forms insight can take. We can directly perceive the ephemeral nature of life through insight into impermanence and change. We can have psychological insights, insights into the nature of our body, and insights into emotions and thought patterns. Insight can manifest as the solution to a problem as we comprehend the web of causal relationships and conditioned patterns influencing our thoughts and behavior. All of these insights can be in service of deepening liberation through nonclinging.

Insights can come on their own as a result of your having calmed your mind, like stilling the wind that ruffles the surface of a lake so you can see the bottom clearly. And you can aim for insights by turning toward any experience to investigate its qualities and how you are relating to what is happening.

You do not have to see farther than you can see. You do not have to know where the process is leading or how to proceed. If you stay open with and receptive to the process as it unfolds, letting what happens guide you organically and using your best judgment for how to meet it, the way forward will reveal itself.

You can be sitting quietly in meditation and an old memory, long forgotten, may suddenly pop into your mind. By staying present with that memory, you may become aware that there is a feeling associated with it. Or perhaps you have a sense, maybe only a vague feeling, of something lying just below the surface of your consciousness. You might hang out with that feeling or memory, or purposefully turn your attention toward it to look closer. You might then notice a body sensation connected with the feeling or memory, maybe tightness in your belly or shoulders or contraction in your heart, and by staying with the feeling in your body you become aware of an emotion. Looking more closely, you remember a painful time from your childhood when you felt unsafe, and how that unsafe feeling has been simmering beneath the surface of your consciousness to this day.

Insights such as these promote deep psychological healing, revealing and loosening the knots of unconscious forces that drive us. In the same way, insight into thought patterns can help us break unconscious clinging and identity. There is not much to a thought. Thoughts seem to come from nowhere, persist for a moment—floating through the mind like the wisp of a cloud—and are gone. Mundane thoughts about buying groceries or remembering an appointment do not bother us. But as insubstantial as they are, when they are not noticed, thoughts of self-criticism and judgment, views and opinions and self-images—they all generate a world of self-view and suffering that we proceed to inhabit as if it were real.

We can easily mistake our critical, judging mind for wise discernment. We believe our thoughts, not seeing that they are our own creation fueled by unconscious habits and patterns. These destructive attitudes and thoughts would not be so detrimental if we could see them for what they are. This is where we need the clarity of insight, because it is only through discernment itself that we learn the difference between judging and discernment.

The critical mind is like a computer program, which only knows how to do one thing, the function for which it is programmed. Clicking on the icon for a word processor will never run a video game. When you click on the computer icons in your mind—when you encounter certain people or situations and the right conditions come together—self-judgment, shame, anger, or fear are set in motion, running through the course of their programming.

The critical mind is not interested in giving you an accurate assessment of yourself or others. It is only interested in carrying out its function: to criticize. And it doesn't care what it lands on; it is happy to land on you or anyone else.

You are the expert on the lived experience of your life. But when you identify with your experience, you may be among the least qualified to judge yourself because you cannot see objectively. You are too caught up, too entangled in your own life to assess it properly. Once, with discernment, you see these forces for what they really are—just conditioned patterns that run through their program when set in motion, you do not have to believe them anymore. They begin to lose their grip on you and ultimately fade away completely.

The Ways Insight Arises

Insights come from within jhana and other meditative states, as a direct result of the deeper stages of samadhi. Insights also come during times in meditation when you cannot concentrate, when it feels like the meditation is not going easily or well, or you are dealing with hindrances and learning how to be present with something difficult or painful. And insights come in the experience of daily activities when you are not meditating at all. Meditation practice serves to support all of these.

Three Marks of All Experience

Insight is traditionally understood as directly perceiving one or more of the three characteristics of all experience: impermanence; the ultimately unsatisfactory nature of all things due to their being impermanent; and the selfless nature of your own being.

When we perceive clearly, not as a concept but as part of our lived experience, that things do not last, we tend not to chase after or cling to them so much, knowing that they are just going to change or be lost. Because all things are changing, if you identify with or cling to anything at all—to having or not having any experience, to your body, your mind, or anything that is bound to change—you either suffer or plant the seeds of future suffering. Knowing directly the suffering that comes from clinging because all things are impermanent helps us to let go. When you start to understand more accurately the nature of your mind and body—the fact that in essence you, too, are a collection of changing experiences—you can rest more at peace within the unfolding of your own being.

We may understand all of this very well conceptually, but we do not live our lives as if it were true. This is why it is so important to perceive these characteristics directly. Ignorance and delusion manifest in many ways. We take what must change as lasting. We seek happiness in what is bound to be lost. And we cling to our minds and bodies, even though we know they are destined to old age, illness, and death. If you cling to your youth you suffer. If you are enslaved to your desires, constantly chasing after pleasant experiences and avoiding the unpleasant ones, you suffer—or set yourself up for future suffering.

Have you ever tried to hold water cupped in your hands? No matter how hard you try, it inevitably drips away through your fingers. Pressing your hands and fingers together more tightly does not help; it hurts, and the water is lost nonetheless. Everything is a changing process. Everything will pass away right through your fingers.

This is not meant to make you sullen or disheartened. Life is not a mistake and nothing is going wrong. It's just the way things are. If you release the grip and stop fighting yourself and the world, it relieves the pain. What you are left with is ease.

Very young children immerse themselves in play, creating whole worlds of trucks and trains, dolls and playhouses. They are deeply engaged and absorbed in their imaginations. As they get older the things that had been so enticing no longer hold any fascination. They did not have to do anything to make this happen; their perceptions gradually shifted, simply as a result of a more mature perspective. What had previously captivated their attention no longer seems of interest and simply drops away on its own.

Just as we lose our fascination with childhood toys as we grow older, when we see how things are, as we begin to understand impermanence and the suffering that comes from trying to hold on to anything, our clinging and suffering start to drop away.

The more deeply we really get it, the more we are able to let go of the subtler places of clinging. When your mind is free from clinging, the pain of pressing your fingers together too tightly stops and an inner peace arises as you allow the water to drip through. The happiness of inner peace is subtler than sense pleasure, but more deeply satisfying. This is a place of stillness, of equanimity, and of peace. In order to know the subtler places of clinging, you need mindfulness, clear awareness, and an undistracted, concentrated mind.

Insight That Arises from Within Samadhi

Stages of deep concentration sharpen the mind's perceptive ability. When you become concentrated your mind is less distracted and naturally more clear and aware. And if you take that to the level of jhana, you attain a level of clarity and undistractedness that was previously inaccessible. Remember what happens in the jhanas. The mind is extremely lucid and undistracted in unbroken mindfulness, with awareness suffused throughout the body.

The more present, awake, and undistracted your mind is, the more clearly it perceives what is most deeply true about your world and yourself: the fact that all conditioned phenomena, all that can be known or sensed, are impermanent and that, as such, they are ultimately unreliable sources of happiness. These insights may come on their own simply as a result of having a concentrated mind, or you can choose to look for these insights within states of samadhi by turning your mind to more deeply investigate and perceive the nature of your body and mind.

Naturally, without your having to do anything, these insights will become clearer. You become increasingly aware of the changing nature of phenomena, recognizing the suffering that comes through clinging, and you come to know more deeply the nature of your heart, mind, and body—the fact that they are also a collection of changing experiences. These insights are great aids in letting go of clinging and helping you rest more equanimously and at peace.

At this stage, the mind has reached a profound degree of clarity in jhana, but things have gotten very still so you have less changing experience to be known by the clear mind. The ability to penetrate into experience has gotten extremely powerful, but the actual experience is so subtle there is not a lot of experience there to penetrate into. The sense of the body can feel quite thin and subtle at this point. You may experience the body dissolving into pure energy or light.

Though it may feel like not much is going on as you rest in the stillness and clarity of mind, you do not need a lot because the power of knowing, seeing, and perceiving is so strong. You penetrate whatever experience there is very clearly and deeply. The characteristics of impermanence and selflessness, the empty nature of the body and the mind, are all directly experienced as a fruit of a concentrated mind. The insights present themselves.

There may be times in jhana or other deep stages of meditation when you choose to consciously, actively turn your mind toward investigation. I have described the mind in jhana as absorbed and undistracted, but while the mind is steady in unbroken mindful knowing there remains part of the mind that you can incline in certain directions. This is a very subtle pointing of awareness, not the gross movements we are used to in ordinary consciousness. You can look for the changing nature of experience, the cause of suffering through clinging, or the nature of your own being.

Insight in Meditation When You Cannot Concentrate

The times when you cannot concentrate, when you are struggling and it feels like the meditation is falling apart, are important for the cultivation of insight—at least as important as the times of extreme clarity in samadhi, and perhaps more so. Our first instinct is to think we have to get back to the good meditation. We think something is going wrong. But nothing is falling apart and nothing is going wrong. There is simply the arising and passing away of the present moment's experience as it has changed. Where there was peace and happiness, now we experience physical pain or emotional stress.

These are special, important times in meditation and we do not want to miss the opportunity for growth they have to offer. If you want to free yourself from suffering then you have to understand your suffering, and if you want to understand your suffering you have to experience the ways your mind creates suffering. If you want to be free, you would rather see your greed, your hatred, and your delusion than not.

You do not have to seek suffering out; it will find you. And when it does, you should appreciate that it is a necessary and important part of the process of insight and welcome the opportunity to change your relationship with the suffering being presented. Watch your mind when you are struggling or suffering in some way. There is a lot of dharma right there in the places where you get caught. That is the place to look—to learn where you cling and how to let it go. That is how the wisdom and insight come in.

Notice how your mind responds to whatever is happening, whether it is resisting or is buffeting around or being reactive in some other way. Watch what is happening. Come to know the suffering quality of a reacting mind. This is a really important place to pay attention. Pay attention to what you do in those times.

Everything you need for learning and growth is there. You experience the First Noble Truth directly, the suffering that arises because of clinging. The Second Noble Truth is illuminated—the fact that it is your craving that is leading you to cling, craving for pleasant experience and wanting to get rid of unpleasant experience. You directly experience what conditions your mind to cling. Everything you need to learn about suffering, its cause, and its cessation presents itself. And you find out whether or not you are yet skillful enough to let go.

Try not to judge the benefit of meditation just by how pleasant or unpleasant it is. Meditation is like riding a bicycle. Think about what it is like riding a bike: You go up and down the hills. Going up can hurt and not be much fun. Going down the hills feels great; you feel the wind and it is easy and pleasant. It feels better going down, but which one do you get the most out of? You get a lot going down from the pleasure and the beauty, but it is the uphill that builds up your endurance and your legs the most.

The path of meditation is sometimes called the path of purification. As you turn your attention inward, connecting deeply and intimately with yourself, parts of you that may have been hidden or covered over begin to be made conscious. Simply by cultivating steady presence, the practice actually brings them up in cycles of purity and purification, and this process only accelerates as you become more collected and settled. In this way, the path of insight and the path of concentration are the same path.

You will enter the deeper stages of samadhi and then will go through cycles or times when it is not so easy, when you do not have the support of the concentration. Rather than react with and push away those experiences, you need to use those times. They serve to unmask levels of clinging you may not have been aware of. You get to find out how you can be with this unpleasant experience and if you can find a way to let go of your suffering around it.

When the hindrances are strong and you cannot find your breath, your ability to work with what is happening can feel feeble, as if you are not really able to practice. It is true that in those times you may not have the strength of clarity and steadiness. But you are practicing fully and well as long as you bring your mindful attention *the best you can* to meet your experience. Just do the best you can; that is enough. Think of how you get good at anything. It is through practice and experience. Learning happens through the struggle; your ability to let go will grow.

Insight in Daily Life

There can be a tendency to view daily life practice as somehow less important than formal meditation. You may think the real benefits come mainly through exceptional states of deep samadhi, but the insights that come in daily life are at least as important as those from the subtle stages of concentration, and perhaps even more so.

There are so many opportunities for insight. You get to find out how you are in relationship to the people at work, family, neighbors, and friends. You get to see when you are able to move through life with a balanced mind and what causes you to close off from situations or people. As you find what helps you live in a balanced way and learn how to let go, there is no disconnection between meditation and any other aspect of your life.

As the fruits of meditation carry into your life you start to notice thoughts and feelings previously covered over by busyness or distraction. It can be alarming when you first begin to wake up to what is really happening in your mind. You begin to see how much of your thoughts are some version of *Am I okay?* or *How am I going to be okay?* or *How am I going to get this?* or *How am I going to avoid that?* By bringing the mindfulness and clear awareness you have been cultivating in formal meditation into ordinary life, it becomes clear how much of your life you spend in peace and fulfillment and how much time is marked by worry or stress.

Dharma practice seeks to shift reactive patterns of grasping and aversion. When your habitual tendencies of chasing your likes and running from your dislikes begin to loosen, you are left to rest peacefully within the ever-changing flow of your life. In order to do this you must come to understand these patterns, and to understand them you have to experience them.

If you want to free yourself from suffering, you need to understand the forces that create suffering responses to life. But you cannot see your conditioning directly. In order to understand these patterns you have to bring them into the light of awareness, and that only happens when the proper neural pathways are activated. The seeds of your reactive habits lie dormant, waiting for the opportunity to sprout when you encounter challenging people, places, and situations. Only under the right circumstances, when certain causes and conditions come together, do they spring forth and grow.

Many of these tendencies only have an opportunity to become conscious in the course of daily activities. You can be sitting in meditation, heart open and mind quiet, happily unbothered by anything because you are secluded from the stresses of your normal interactions. Then you get up from meditation to begin your day and encounter a person you dislike or hear a news story that upsets you.

You gain valuable insights into the ways you fall into reactivity or where your heart closes off, opening you to the possibility of freedom. See them as the opportunity for learning how to live in equanimity with a peaceful mind and an open heart.

Chapter 10

EQUANIMITY

The entire teaching of the Buddha can be viewed as making a radical shift in how we seek happiness—a shift that has far-reaching and profound consequences for our well-being. This process of transforming our relationship with our life and ourselves culminates in a mind of inner peace and nonreactive presence, a state of equanimity.

Without equanimity we tend to meet situations through unseen filters of reactivity, causing us to deny our experience or pull away from anything we dislike or chase after what we want. When you are balanced you neither push away nor cling; you don't suppress your feelings or thoughts, but you also don't get caught in or identified with them. Between reactions of grasping and aversion lies the freedom to choose your own way, how you will relate and respond to life.

Equanimity is both the path and the fruit of the path. You employed equanimity the first time you sat to meditate as you tried to let go of grasping and aversion and sit quietly with yourself. You may have felt tenuous and unsteady, but you did the best you could and it was enough. Through those initial efforts equanimity matured and your capacity for meeting your experience grew. As you became increasingly able to turn toward and work with whatever arose in meditation, mindfulness and steadiness grew.

It can seem so hard to live with a peaceful mind, an open heart, and compassion for others and ourselves. Equanimity acts as an ally, support, and shield against the "eight worldly concerns" of gain and loss, fame and disrepute, praise and blame, and pleasure and pain. These four pairs of opposites are powerful incentives driving most human behavior. We are constantly judging and comparing ourselves and our situations. You can appreciate success, but if your sense of well-being depends on it you are setting yourself up for disappointment when the situation changes. If you are attached to honor and approval, it may feel good until you are faced with criticism. If you become egotistical, your self-worth can be based on comparing yourself to others. The more deeply you identify with your successes, the more profoundly you will identify with failure.

With equanimity you remain unshaken. Your peace and happiness are not left to chance forces outside your control and you remain independent, gliding over the bumps of life's ups and downs.

Equanimity should not be mistaken for passivity. It does not mean you are no longer engaged in life or should stop trying to change your circumstances when appropriate. But you should do all this from wisdom, not from reactivity. If you think you are supposed to stay with something when it really is too much to deal with, you fall into struggle.

An acorn will eventually grow into a great oak tree, able to withstand powerful storms. When the sapling is small it is weak and vulnerable, so one builds a fence to protect it and guard against animals or wind. There is no need for a fence once the tree has matured. Until equanimity is well developed, you are more easily blown by the winds of bother or stress. As wisdom grows and your boundary point moves out, your heart and mind can rest freely in the midst of ever more turmoil. Until then you must find a way to back off or bring down the intensity to within a range in which you can work.

Stress can be defined as the gap between your experience and your ability to be fully present in the midst of that experience without struggle. The wider the gap, the more you suffer. Equanimity means closing the gap. We create suffering through our inability to be with life as it is, and through our aversion to unpleasant, unwanted experiences. There is no problem if we do not think life is supposed to be any way other than it is.

The Buddha expressed this using an analogy. He said both the ordinary and the enlightened person experience the full range of physical and mental processes, all the pleasant and unpleasant feelings available through the senses. Both experience the unpleasantness of painful physical sensations, which the Buddha likened to being struck by an arrow. The ordinary person then creates another extra layer of suffering, in addition to the painful experience itself, by clinging to the pleasant or fighting against the unpleasant. This, said the Buddha, is like being struck by a second arrow, whereas the enlightened person, for whom there is no gap, is struck only once.

Ending Destructive Impulses

The equanimity of the Buddha is described as a destruction of three fundamental forces that lead to reactivity and stress. When these deeply conditioned patterns are no longer operational, you will have arrived in a state of balance and inner peace beyond any method or technique.

These three tendencies of mind are closely related and reinforce each other. The first of these is ignorance, not understanding the truth of suffering, its cause, its cessation, and the way leading to its cessation: the Four Noble Truths. The insight into suffering that dispels ignorance is beyond mere intellectual understanding; it is an immediate knowing that manifests moment by moment within the reality of your life.

When immersed in our pursuits we cannot see the tension or anxiety that may be right in front of us. We experience a lack, a sense of something missing, or we are unable to let go of our aversion to whatever is difficult or painful. Always seeking satisfaction in the next great experience, we are so caught we cannot see the stress inherent in looking for happiness outside our self. It is due to ignorance that we do not perceive the suffering inherent in giving our well-being over to whether or not our experience is to our liking. Once we begin to wake up more fully to what is happening, to what is right in front of us, we directly experience the clinging that comes from craving, and the suffering that ensues.

The second tendency that destroys equanimity, seeking happiness by fulfilling sense pleasures, comes directly from ignorance. There is little or nothing we do that is not an effort to increase pleasant feelings and to decrease or avoid unpleasant feelings. This fundamental motivating force to seek happiness and avoid pain is deeply ingrained in our conditioning.

It may seem counterintuitive that seeking happiness by fulfilling desires does not work in the long term and, in fact, creates precisely the suffering we are trying to avoid. But gratifying desire rarely delivers its promise of happiness. It may elevate us momentarily to a state of satisfaction and contentment—certainly there can be the immediate pleasure of fulfilling desire—but once the initial excitement or pleasure wears off, we are left back in our usual, ordinary state of mind.

Desires seduce us by their promise of happiness, by the anticipation that by satisfying them we will feel more fulfilled. We believe that if we could only discover the right things to go after, and then apply ourselves properly to the task of getting them, we could attain some sort of enduring happiness that until now has escaped us.

In addition to making our happiness dependent upon circumstance and creating, at best, a temporary happiness destined to change, seeking happiness by fulfilling desire conditions the mind for further craving. The objects of our desire can be difficult to secure; once acquired they often provide less pleasure or happiness than expected; and when clung to they cause us grief when conditions inevitably change. Then, feeling empty or in need, we are once again driven to repeat the cycle.

How many desires have you filled and how often have you filled them, only to have them return, putting you on a constant treadmill, always having to satisfy them again? Alleviating the cravings associated with desire by fulfilling desire is like drinking seawater to alleviate thirst: it can be a great relief for a short while, since for the time being it eases the suffering inherent in craving, but it has the more fundamental effect of conditioning the mind to crave more. We are satiated for a while until the next craving, often for the same object or experience of the previous desire.

The third force aiming us away from equanimity is called "becoming." It is the drive to be something. It is not that you need to stop having a mind, a body, and a personality. It is *having* to be something, and clinging to an identity through which you judge and compare yourself to others, that plants the seeds of suffering.

Just as the potential for sense pleasure to bring lasting happiness is limited, clinging to an identity is not a reliable way to inner peace. If you are identified with your youth, you suffer when youth and beauty fade. If you are identified with your achievements, job title, or role, or to the opinions of others, your peace of mind is in the hands of forces outside your control.

You do not have to stop living. You can continue to be involved with those things that bring you meaning—work life, family or friends, creative expression, and involvement in the affairs of the world. The shift is in your priorities, where you look for meaning and happiness, and in the motivating principles upon which your life is based. As you move forward in life, to the extent you are consumed by your goals and bound up in having to have them, your happiness and well-being are dependent upon them and you will suffer when they are not realized or when the situation inevitably changes.

With a mind of equanimity, you find the balance between being connected and engaged in your life without clinging to any of it.

Becoming Disentangled

Equanimity is often misunderstood as being a state of indifference. We may think we are supposed to be detached witnesses removed from the concerns of others or the world. But equanimity does not mean being numb or untouched by anything, or that no feelings can arise.

Equanimity means remaining poised and centered within whatever happens. The ability to let go has nothing to do with being unfeeling or unconcerned about others, and everything to do with meeting life with balance and composure.

The ability to let go comes through disenchantment and dispassion. Disenchantment can carry a negative connotation, conveying a sense of being disappointed or let down. If people invested time and effort into something and it did not work out, we may say they gave up and moved on to a new endeavor because they became disenchanted or disillusioned.

But disenchantment does not mean disappointment. It means to be free from enchantment. To be disillusioned does not mean to be let down. It is to be no longer caught in illusion. In the old fairy tales when a sorcerer casts a spell people become enchanted. They no longer have a sense of reality and are enmeshed in a spellbound world of confusion. Once the spell is broken and they are no longer enchanted, they see the world as it really is. Only then have they reconnected with reality.

Similarly, dispassion can connote a feeling of impassivity or indifference. But dispassion does not mean you are detached from yourself or those around you. If you are passionate about something or someone you are tied to them with strong emotions or desires. You are not only interested or committed; you are swept up in the intoxicating allure of those emotions and desires. To be dispassionate means you are no longer ruled by the passions or caught up emotionally. If you say to loved ones that you are detached from them, it probably is not going to be received very well. If you tell them you are not clinging to them, they will probably appreciate it.

Humans are hardwired to attach. It is built into our DNA. Infants must attach to a primary caregiver or they will not thrive.

Healthy attachment is an essential part of early childhood development, and those with ambivalent attachment as children may find it hard to form satisfying relationships as adults, or may face other psychological or emotional issues.

We are not aiming to disconnect. In fact, we are doing the opposite—connecting with our bodies and minds profoundly, beyond the surface appearance normally accessible. Reflect on how you have been meditating. You close your eyes and draw your attention inward. You cultivate mindfulness and concentration, and turn that clear, undistracted awareness directly toward connecting deeply with your body and mind.

An equanimous mind is open to all of life, including all parts of you. It does not suppress anything. By now you have seen how beautiful your mind can be, and you may also have touched places within that you wished were not there. There is no experience you are supposed to have or not have. This is a path of connecting with yourself, deeply and profoundly, but remaining *disentangled* in the midst of it all.

Many people find that as equanimity matures they are more interested in the lives of others and the world around them than ever before. When you are not consumed by the eight worldly concerns, you are not preoccupied with yourself. When you are not reacting to a situation, you are able to be more present and connected, not less. Rather than feeling detached, you find yourself able to open to and be present with all sorts of situations and people. A mind of equanimity is not consumed with what it can get, but is deeply interested in what it can give.

Factors Supporting Equanimity

The dharma qualities that support and grow from meditation are like sides of a multifaceted jewel, each reflecting and magnifying light from all the other surfaces, the rays feeding back on each other in a positive reinforcing cycle. Any one of them is an access point for the others.

Intention

All along we have emphasized the central role intention plays in the course of dharma practice. Especially in those times when you are pulled by forces of desire, negativity, or doubt, keeping in mind wholesome intentions for how you want to live and act provides a refuge, helping you stay balanced through the many challenges and rewards of a meditative life. Rather than being caught up and swept along by a situation, the clarity of your intention acts as a touchstone, anchoring you in wise and skillful action.

Virtue

All of your actions are born from intentions, whether you are aware of them or not. Out of your sincere, wholesome intentions comes virtuous action. By aiming to live with integrity you dwell peacefully with others, and when your interactions are harmonious your mind is not agitated by conflict. This leads to a quiet confidence in knowing there is a blameless quality to your life.

Gladdening Your Mind

Living virtuously in alignment with your intentions, you are more happy and at peace. It is reassuring to know you are on a positive track, using your time well by aiming to create less suffering and more well-being for others and yourself. You feel the goodness of your intentions and the happiness of knowing you have put those intentions into action. Being reassured leads to relaxation and ease, and when you are at ease, not stressed or worried, you feel a sense of balance and calm.

Mindfulness

Mindfulness provides a space between what happens and your response to it. Within that space rests the freedom to decide whether you will react on impulse or respond through wisdom. It is a moment of choice in the midst of any situation. With mindfulness, when equanimity is present you know it. When you are thrown off balance you know that, and can employ the tools you have built to help you regain composure.

Steadiness

As concentration becomes established, equanimity is not so easily shaken. Concentration strings moments of mindfulness together. You can go for long periods caught up in life, going through the motions unaware of what you are doing. But if you maintain a state of steady undistractedness throughout the day, you become increasingly awake to the present moment.

Discernment

Supported by mindfulness and steadiness, you begin to see things as they are without getting caught up in stories about them. You have the experience to choose the appropriate tools and apply them skillfully in any situation. As patterns of reactivity are recognized through mindfulness and steady presence, the knots of aversion and stress, desire and attachment, begin to unravel. You are naturally open to more happiness, contentment, compassion, wisdom, and peace.

Finding the Teacher Within

Regardless of your situation, you can begin cultivating a quiet mind and an open, compassionate heart. With intention you can start to use your time more wisely for mindfully connecting with your experience in order to explore the potential for freedom within your life circumstances. With practice you begin, bit by bit, to awaken to and live more fully in alliance with your own inner wisdom.

There comes a time when you are no longer a seeker. You will have arrived at a place of knowing and being, the confluence of the path and the goal.

This is not an egotistical place, in which you think you have learned all there is to know and no one can tell you anything. It is not saying there is no longer a path to follow or no further work to be done. We cannot see our own blind spots. It would be a mistake to think you never need the guidance and advice of those who have traveled further along the path. We do not want to become arrogant or complacent, thinking we do not need mentors. Otherwise we risk running into unnecessary cul-de-sacs or bad neighborhoods that would be better avoided altogether.

Ultimately, we go from being students to becoming our own teacher. As the dharma comes alive in you, you will have less need to rely on any outside authority. With time and experience you will learn to trust your own inner guidance. Your experience will be your guide. The times, in any situation, when you clearly know what is happening and it is obvious what to do, will increase. You will not need to look outside of yourself.

The person who splashes in the shallows of the ocean does not find the pearls. If you want to understand you have to dive deeply, and then you will find them. Through meditation you open to the deeper truths of yourself and the world around you. You go from being a seeker to resting in the stream of knowing and being, as you learn to live equanimously with a quiet mind and an open heart.

Richard Shankman has been a meditator since 1970, and teaches at Dharma centers and groups internationally. He is guiding teacher of the Metta Dharma Foundation, and cofounder of the Sati Center for Buddhist Studies and of Mindful Schools. Shankman is author of *The Experience of Samadhi*.

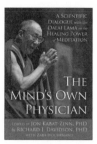
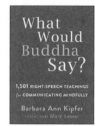

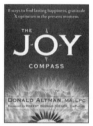
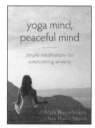

DARK TRUTH

SUPERMAN/WONDER WOMAN

VOLUME 4
DARK TRUTH

WRITTEN BY
PETER J. TOMASI

PENCILS BY
DOUG MAHNKE
ARDIAN SYAF
TOM DERENICK

INKS BY
JAIME MENDOZA
RAY McCARTHY
JONATHAN GLAPION
MARC DEERING
SEAN PARSONS
MARK IRWIN
SCOTT HANNA
JOHNNY DESJARDINS
KEITH CHAMPAGNE
TOM DERENICK
JORDI TARRAGONA

COLOR BY
WIL QUINTANA
ULISES ARREOLA
TOMEU MOREY

LETTERS BY
ROB LEIGH
TRAVIS LANHAM
TOM NAPOLITANO

COLLECTION COVER ART BY
CARY NORD

SUPERMAN CREATED BY
JERRY SIEGEL &
JOE SHUSTER
BY SPECIAL ARRANGEMENT
WITH THE JERRY SIEGEL FAMILY

WONDER WOMAN CREATED BY
WILLIAM MOULTON MARSTON

SUPERMAN/WONDER WOMAN

EDDIE BERGANZA Editor – Original Series
ANDREW MARINO JEREMY BENT Assistant Editors – Original Series
JEB WOODARD Group Editor – Collected Editions
SUZANNAH ROWNTREE Editor – Collected Edition
STEVE COOK Design Director – Books
DAMIAN RYLAND Publication Design

BOB HARRAS Senior VP – Editor-in-Chief, DC Comics

DIANE NELSON President
DAN DiDIO Publisher
JIM LEE Publisher
GEOFF JOHNS President & Chief Creative Officer
AMIT DESAI Executive VP – Business & Marketing Strategy, Direct to Consumer & Global Franchise Management
SAM ADES Senior VP – Direct to Consumer
BOBBIE CHASE VP – Talent Development
MARK CHIARELLO Senior VP – Art, Design & Collected Editions
JOHN CUNNINGHAM Senior VP – Sales & Trade Marketing
ANNE DePIES Senior VP – Business Strategy, Finance & Administration
DON FALLETTI VP – Manufacturing Operations
LAWRENCE GANEM VP – Editorial Administration & Talent Relations
ALISON GILL Senior VP – Manufacturing & Operations
HANK KANALZ Senior VP – Editorial Strategy & Administration
JAY KOGAN VP – Legal Affairs
THOMAS LOFTUS VP – Business Affairs
JACK MAHAN VP – Business Affairs
NICK J. NAPOLITANO VP – Manufacturing Administration
EDDIE SCANNELL VP – Consumer Marketing
COURTNEY SIMMONS Senior VP – Publicity & Communications
JIM (SKI) SOKOLOWSKI VP – Comic Book Specialty Sales & Trade Marketing
NANCY SPEARS VP – Mass, Book, Digital Sales & Trade Marketing

SUPERMAN/WONDER WOMAN VOLUME 4: DARK TRUTH

DC Comics, 2900 West Alameda Ave., Burbank, CA 91505
Printed by LSC Communications, Salem, VA, USA. 11/18/16. First Printing.
ISBN: 978-1-4012-6544-1

Library of Congress Cataloging-in-Publication Data

Names: Tomasi, Peter, author. | Mahnke, Doug, illustrator.
Title: Superman/Wonder Woman. Volume 4, Dark truth / Peter J. Tomasi, writer
; Doug Mahnke, artist.
Other titles: Dark truth
Description: Burbank, CA : DC Comics, [2016]
Identifiers: LCCN 2016006922 | ISBN 978-1-4012-6544-1
Subjects: LCSH: Graphic novels. | Superhero comic books, strips, etc. |
BISAC: COMICS & GRAPHIC NOVELS / Superheroes.
Classification: LCC PN6728.S9 T67 2016 | DDC 741.5/973–dc23
LC record available at http://lccn.loc.gov/2016006922

PEFC Certified

Printed on paper from
sustainably managed
forests, controlled
sources

PEFC
PEFC/29-31-337   www.pefc.org

DARK TRUTH PART ONE

PETER J. TOMASI writer DOUG MAHNKE penciller JAIME MENDOZA RAY MCCARTHY JONATHAN GLAPION MARC DEERING inkers WIL QUINTANA colorist

ROB LEIGH letterer cover by PAULO SIQUEIRA & HI-FI

A FRIENDSHIP FORGED.

OUR LOVE BORN.

NEW POWER REALIZED AND OTHERS TAKEN AWAY.

HIS SECRET REVEALED.

SO MUCH, SO FAST.

FINDING RESPITE WHERE WE CAN.

FROM THE TEMPEST OF CHANGE ALL AROUND US.

I AM HIS SENTINEL...

...AND NO HARM WILL COME TO MY LOVE WHILE I DRAW BREATH.

DARK TRUTH

CLARK, IT'S THREE A.M., YOU HAVE A PHONE CALL. SMALLVILLE AREA CODE. WAKE UP.

...I'M UP... I'M UP...

LANA-- WHAT IS IT-- EVERYTHING ALL RIGHT?

--SOMEONE OR SOMETHING'S IN MY PARENTS' HOUSE--

--THEY'VE DONE SOMETHING TO JOHN AND THEY'RE--

LANA-- ARE YOU--

CLARK? TALK TO ME. WHAT'S GOING ON?

SMALLVILLE.

I NEED TO GET TO SMALLVILLE, DIANA.

NOW.

THEN WHAT ARE WE WAITING FOR?

REMEMBER, IF ONE OF US CAN FLY...

DIANA-- PLEASE-- GO FASTER.

BUT YOUR BODY AND LUNGS-- WITH YOUR POWERS NOT AT FULL STRENGTH-- CAN THEY HANDLE THE SPEED AND AIR PRESSURE?

I DON'T CARE, EVERY MINUTE COUNTS.

I CAN'T LET HER DOWN AGAIN.

I WON'T.

WHO WON'T YOU LET DOWN AGAIN?

THE "BIG RED" ON YOUR PHONE SCREEN?

LANA LANG.

MY FIRST REAL GIRLFRIEND...

...SHE HELPED ME DEAL WITH MY POWERS.

AND WAS MY ROCK WHEN MY PARENTS DIED.

SHE KNEW YOU WERE SUPERMAN ALL THESE YEARS?

YEAH...

...WAY BEFORE THE REST OF THE PLANET FOUND OUT.

SOUNDS LIKE SHE REALLY MEANS A LOT TO YOU.

SOMEONE I LOOK FORWARD TO MEETING.

WE'VE BEEN HERE ALMOST FIFTEEN MINUTES, DAMN IT...

...DOESN'T MAKE SENSE. THERE'S NOT ONE SIGN OF A STRUGGLE...

...ESPECIALLY SINCE HER BOYFRIEND, *JOHN HENRY IRONS*, WAS WITH HER.

HE WOULDN'T HAVE GONE DOWN WITHOUT A FIGHT--AND ON TOP OF HIM BEING *STEEL*, THERE WOULD'VE BEEN SOME MAJOR DAMAGE.

NOTHING'S OUT OF PLACE... IT'S LIKE IT'S...

TOO PERFECT.

DOESN'T EVEN SEEM LIVED IN, ESPECIALLY IF LANA AND IRONS WERE USING THE HOUSE.

YOU SAID A FEW MINUTES AGO LANA'S ELECTRICAL ENGINEERING JOB PUT HER ON THE ROAD A LOT.

DO YOU KNOW WHY SHE WAS HERE IN SMALLVILLE NOW?

LAST WE SPOKE SHE WAS COMING TO SETTLE UP HER PARENTS' ESTATE PLANNING AFTER...

...I WASN'T ABLE TO SAVE THEM FROM THE DOOMSDAY VIRUS.

YOU SEEM SO COMFORTABLE HERE, CLARK.

THERE'S A PART OF ME THAT WISHES YOU NEVER LEFT.

DEALING WITH THE CRAZINESS OF MY POWERS BACK THEN... SEEMS LIKE SUCH A SIMPLER TIME COMPARED TO WHAT'S HAPPENING NOW...

WHERE THE HELL IS SHE?!?

SKRAKK

IT'S OKAY.

WE'LL FIND LANA AND IRONS.

OUR NEXT STEP IS TO HEAD INTO SMALLVILLE AND GATHER MORE INTEL.

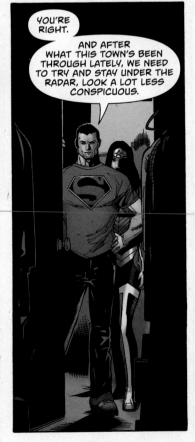

YOU'RE RIGHT.

AND AFTER WHAT THIS TOWN'S BEEN THROUGH LATELY, WE NEED TO TRY AND STAY UNDER THE RADAR, LOOK A LOT LESS CONSPICUOUS.

WHERE WE HEADING?

THE BARBERSHOP.

THE THREE WISE MEN OUT FRONT KNOW ALL THE COMINGS AND GOINGS IN THIS TOWN...

MORNING, GENTLEMEN.

HEY THERE, CLARK.

WHO'S YOUR FRIEND?

DIANA.

DIDN'T THINK WE'D BE SEEING YOU SO SOON, WHAT WITH THE RECENT...REVELATIONS.

THERE'S IMPORTANT REASONS, BURT, WHY I COULDN'T TELL YOU ALL ABOUT BEING...

SUPERMAN. IT'S OKAY TO SAY IT OUT LOUD NOW, CLARK.

AND I PROMISE I WILL AT SOME POINT, BUT RIGHT NOW LANA'S MISSING AND--

SHE'S ONE OF MANY.

WHAT--WHO ELSE, MR. LANDERS?

WELL, AS YOU CAN SEE, SANTIAGO ISN'T KEEPING HIS USUAL CHAIR WARM, AND MRS. TAKAHARA DIDN'T MAKE IT INTO SCHOOL THIS MORNING EITHER, ALONG WITH A FEW OTHERS.

GOT US A TOWN HALL TONIGHT TO BEND SOME EARS AND FLAP SOME LIPS.

LOOK, WE'RE **NOT** SAYING WE DON'T TRUST YOU ANYMORE, CAUSE WE DO.

AND WE DON'T CARE WHERE YOU CAME FROM.

ONLY A FOOL CAN'T SEE THAT KEEPING PEOPLE SAFE IS WHAT YOU CARE MOST ABOUT.

YEAH, IT'S BEEN EASY TO SEE EVEN FROM WHEN YOU WERE A KID THAT YOU'VE GOT THE EYES AND HEART OF A GOOD MAN.

BUT ONE THING WE DO KNOW IS THAT A HELLUVA LOT OF BAD MOJO'S BEEN FOLLOWING YOU AROUND LATELY...

AND AS MUCH AS IT PAINS US TO EVEN SPEAK THESE WORDS...WELL...I THINK PUTTING SOME SPACE BETWEEN YOU AND SMALLVILLE IS WHAT'S BEST FOR THE FOLKS IN THIS TOWN RIGHT NOW, CLARK.

DOOMSDAY, BRAINIAC, ULTRA-HUMANITE...YOU'RE A TARGET AND IN TURN YOU'RE MAKING US A TARGET.

DON'T YOU THINK WE'VE EARNED SOME PEACE AND QUIET AROUND HERE, CLARK?

I DO, AND I COMPLETELY UNDERSTAND WHERE YOU'RE COMING FROM, MISTER LANDERS.

I'LL GET **OUR** PEOPLE BACK.

THEY **TOOK** IT ALL.

MY PARENTS' HOME...

...THE BARN...

...EVERYTHING...

...LIKE **MY FAMILY** WAS NEVER HERE.

SKRRUNCH

AND IF THEY RIPPED AWAY **THIS** LAND THERE'S A GOOD CHANCE...

Hmm.

THEY TORE *THIS* AWAY, TOO.

FUMPP

INITIATE PROTOCOL AC638.

WHOSE LAND IS THIS?

WASHINGTON AND EMILY KENT-- GRANDPARENTS ON MY FATHER'S SIDE.

THEY DIED IN A CAR ACCIDENT WHEN I WAS TWELVE.

MY PARENTS SOLD THE LAND A LITTLE LATER.

I'M *NOT* SANCTIONING THE PROTOCOL WITHOUT AN EXECUTIVE AUDIO AND PRESENT-DAY PASSWORD CONFIRMATION.

ON ITS WAY SHORTLY.

WELL, IF IT'S *NOT*, THE HORSES STAY IN THE BARN, UNDERSTOOD?

OF COURSE.

EVERYONE AND EVERYTHING I'VE BEEN *CLOSE TO* HERE IN SMALLVILLE'S BEEN PUT AT RISK.

GENERATIONS OF KENTS POURED THEIR HEARTS AND SOULS INTO THIS LAND...

KLANKK

...AND NOW *THEIR* LEGACY IS TAINTED BECAUSE OF *MY* CHOICES.

BUT WHATEVER COVERT DEPARTMENT THE GOVERNMENT SENT IN TO PROBE MY LIFE...

WHAMM

...ENDED UP MISSING THIS. MY GRANDFATHER'S BOMB SHELTER.

HEARD HIS THOUGHTS ABOUT WHERE THIS WORLD WAS GOING RAN A LITTLE DARK.

YOUR KRYPTONIAN FATHER, JOR-EL, AND HE WOULD'VE GOTTEN ALONG WELL.

NO ONE EVEN KNEW ABOUT THIS SHELTER-- NOT MY PARENTS OR THE PEOPLE WHO BOUGHT THE LAND FROM THEM.

KEPT COMING HERE WITHOUT THE NEW OWNERS EVER FINDING OUT.

THIS WAS YOUR SAFE PLACE, WASN'T IT, CLARK?

WHERE YOU CAME TO GET AWAY FROM IT ALL.

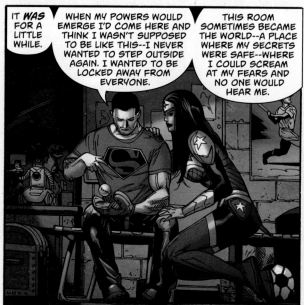

IT **WAS** FOR A LITTLE WHILE.

WHEN MY POWERS WOULD EMERGE I'D COME HERE AND THINK I WASN'T SUPPOSED TO BE LIKE THIS--I NEVER WANTED TO STEP OUTSIDE AGAIN. I WANTED TO BE LOCKED AWAY FROM EVERYONE.

THIS ROOM SOMETIMES BECAME THE WORLD--A PLACE WHERE MY SECRETS WERE SAFE--WHERE I COULD SCREAM AT MY FEARS AND NO ONE WOULD HEAR ME.

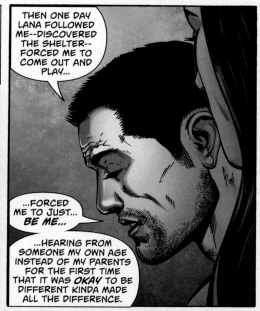

THEN ONE DAY LANA FOLLOWED ME--DISCOVERED THE SHELTER--FORCED ME TO COME OUT AND PLAY...

...FORCED ME TO JUST... **BE ME**...

...HEARING FROM SOMEONE MY OWN AGE INSTEAD OF MY PARENTS FOR THE FIRST TIME THAT IT WAS **OKAY** TO BE DIFFERENT KINDA MADE ALL THE DIFFERENCE.

YOU KNOW, AS WE WERE LANDING I THOUGHT MAYBE SHE ESCAPED, MADE IT HERE...

...BUT WHEN I DIDN'T SEE FOOTPRINTS IN THE DIRT LEADING UP TO THE SHELTER DOOR, I REALIZED THAT WASN'T--

CLARK-- WHAT IS IT?

THIS WASN'T THEIR LAST STOP.

FIRST ULTRA-HUMANITE DIGS MY PARENTS UP--DESECRATES THEIR BODIES--

--NOW THIS.

C'MON, I'M STANDING RIGHT HERE!

WHAT ARE YOU WAITING FOR, DAMN IT!

BUDDABUDDABUDDABUDDABUDDA

DARK TRUTH PART TWO

PETER J. TOMASI writer **DOUG MAHNKE** penciller **JAIME MENDOZA** inker **WIL QUINTANA** colorist **ROB LEIGH** letterer
cover by **DOUG MAHNKE, JAIME MENDOZA & WIL QUINTANA**

JUSTICE

SMALLVILLE CEMETERY, KANSAS.

WHAT DO *YOU* WANT HERE?

WE WERE TOLD TO RUMBLE TUMBLE, SO LET'S GET TO IT.

WHY?

OURS IS NOT TO QUESTION WHY.

YEAH, OURS IS BUT TO DO OR *DIE*.

HA. YOU COULD CALL US A--

DARK TRUTH

PART TWO

FUNNY.

I WAS JUST THINKING THE SAME THING ABOUT YOU.

UNFF

WHAMM

KOOM KOOM

KOOM! KOOM!

KOOM

KOOM

FINISHED?

YEAH.

GOOD.

ME, TOO.

SOMEONE HERE'S GOT TO HAVE INTEL WE CAN USE.

WELL, IF WE LEFT SOMEONE *CONSCIOUS*, THAT WOULD'VE HELPED.

...UHH...

I GUESS WE DID, AFTER ALL.

WHERE HAVE THEY TAKEN THE PEOPLE FROM SMALLVILLE, MANTA?

...DON'T KNOW... WHAT YOU'RE... TALKING ABOUT...

WHY ARE YOU COMING AT ME LIKE THIS?

DON'T YOU KNOW... IT'S OPEN SEASON...ON SUPERMAN.

WHAT *I* KNOW IS YOU MADE ME *VERY* UNHAPPY!

SKRRKK

...NOT EXACTLY THE *SUPERMAN*... WE'VE ALL COME TO KNOW, *KENT*...

THINGS CHANGE.

CLARK, WE'RE WASTING TIME HERE, WE SHOULD--

A CHANGE HAS COME. THROWN EVERYTHING OFF-KILTER IN SUCH A...DRASTIC WAY THAT WE'LL NEED TO FIGURE OUT HOW--

YOU HAVE TO DO SOMETHING FOR ME.

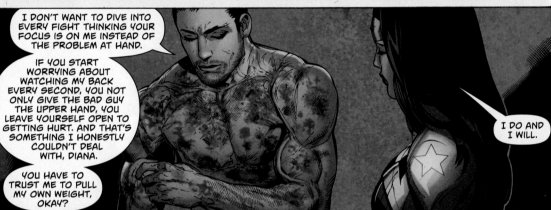

I DON'T WANT TO DIVE INTO EVERY FIGHT THINKING YOUR FOCUS IS ON ME INSTEAD OF THE PROBLEM AT HAND.

IF YOU START WORRYING ABOUT WATCHING MY BACK EVERY SECOND, YOU NOT ONLY GIVE THE BAD GUY THE UPPER HAND, YOU LEAVE YOURSELF OPEN TO GETTING HURT. AND THAT'S SOMETHING I HONESTLY COULDN'T DEAL WITH, DIANA.

YOU HAVE TO TRUST ME TO PULL MY OWN WEIGHT, OKAY?

I DO AND I WILL.

DO YOU EVER FEEL LIKE WE'RE JUST SOLDIERS?

STANDING UP AGAINST MONSTERS AND PROTECTING PEOPLE WHO CAN'T PROTECT THEMSELVES.

AND IN A STRANGE WAY...

...I FEEL LIKE ONE MORE THAN EVER NOW THAT I'M VULNERABLE TO A THIRTY-CENT PIECE OF METAL.

C'MON, WHAT ARE YOU THINKING ABOUT?

WITH YOUR POWER LEVELS CHANGING--MAYBE THIS ISN'T THE BASELINE...

WHAT IF YOU GET EVEN WEAKER?

GUESS WE'LL CROSS THAT BRIDGE WHEN AND IF WE COME TO IT.

I DON'T WANT TO LOSE YOU.

YOU WON'T.

THESE BULLETS DEADSHOT USED... SPECIALLY CRAFTED, A STRANGE CALIBER...

WHAT IF IT'S JUST THE BEGINNING...

KRRNK

...WHAT IF THEY'RE BUILDING SOMETHING EVEN DEADLIER... SOMETHING EVEN BIGGER THAT CAN TAKE YOU DOWN?

I'M NOT WORRIED ABOUT ME.

I'M WORRIED ABOUT LANA AND THE OTHERS.

THE REPERCUSSIONS OF ALL THIS--

--HAS FORCED MY HAND.

I NEED TO TAKE A TRIP.

KRRK

PLIKK

SORRY.

...THAT'S WHY I REACHED OUT TO YOU.

I KNOW HOW IT CAN BE PERCEIVED, BUT IN THE END I THINK IT'LL HELP CLARIFY THINGS AND RECTIFY AT LEAST THAT SPECIFIC SITUATION.

KNOK KNOK

YES, COME IN. WHAT IS IT?

I'LL TELL YOU, MR. PRESIDENT...

DARK TRUTH PART THREE

PETER J. TOMASI writer DOUG MAHNKE penciller JAIME MENDOZA SEAN PARSONS inkers WIL QUINTANA colorist
ROB LEIGH letterer cover by PAULO SIQUEIRA & HI-FI

I'M IN
O MOOD FOR
SHELL GAME,
TREVOR.
I NEED TO SPEAK WITH HIM.
DID YOU REALLY THINK ONCE WE TRACKED YOU HEADING TO D.C. THAT WE'D ALLOW THE LEADER OF THE FREE WORLD TO GREET YOU WITHOUT TAKING SOME PRECAUTIONS?
AND DID YOU REALLY THINK I'D HARM THE PRESIDENT?
I DON'T HAVE THE LUXURY AT THIS TIME TO ASSUME ANYTHING, SUPERMAN.
OR SHOULD I SAY, CLARK KENT?
DARK TRUTH
PART THREE
A MATTER OF TRUST

I EXPECTED THE PRESIDENT TO BE SITTING HERE, *NOT* AN A.R.G.U.S. AGENT.

I'M *HERE* BECAUSE THE ENTIRE COUNTRY--NOT TO MENTION THE REST OF THE WORLD--IS A LITTLE ON EDGE AFTER *THE DAILY PLANET* DROPPED ITS SECRET-IDENTITY BOMBSHELL.

AND *I'M HERE* BECAUSE WHAT WENT DOWN IN SMALLVILLE'S UNACCEPTABLE AND--

--IS EXACTLY WHAT LOIS LANE'S ARTICLE FORCED US TO DO.

YOU WEREN'T *FORCED* TO DO ANYTHING EXCEPT MAKE A CONSCIOUS CHOICE TO TEAR INNOCENT PEOPLE OUT OF THEIR HOMES AND OUT OF THEIR LIVES.

THINGS HAVE BECOME SOMEWHAT... BLURRY...

...WHICH, IF YOU HAVEN'T GUESSED BY NOW, FORCES THE POWERS THAT BE TO SUDDENLY FOCUS AND BATTEN DOWN THE HATCHES.

YOU DO REALIZE YOU'RE GIVING ME THE *SECOND* BIGGEST STORY OF THE YEAR!

LAST I CHECKED, THE ADVANCED RESEARCH GROUP UNITING SUPER-HUMANS IS PART OF THE POWERS THAT BE.

THEY TOOK *MY* CAMERA.

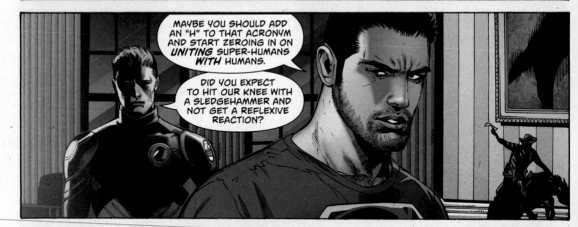

MAYBE YOU SHOULD ADD AN "H" TO THAT ACRONYM AND START ZEROING IN ON *UNITING* SUPER-HUMANS *WITH* HUMANS.

DID YOU EXPECT TO HIT OUR KNEE WITH A SLEDGEHAMMER AND NOT GET A REFLEXIVE REACTION?

...TWENTY...

...TWENTY-ONE...

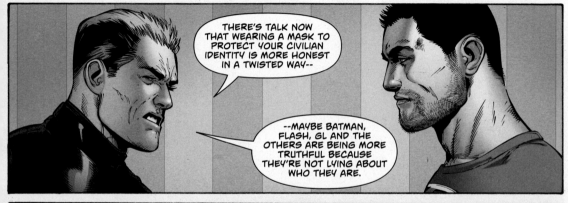

THERE'S TALK NOW THAT WEARING A MASK TO PROTECT YOUR CIVILIAN IDENTITY IS MORE HONEST IN A TWISTED WAY--

--MAYBE BATMAN, FLASH, GL AND THE OTHERS ARE BEING MORE TRUTHFUL BECAUSE THEY'RE NOT LYING ABOUT WHO THEY ARE.

BRATTABRATTA

AND WORST OF ALL, IT EVEN MAKES PEOPLE DOUBT DIANA, AQUAMAN AND CYBORG. IS THERE AN ULTERIOR MOTIVE FOR THEM *NOT* WEARING MASKS, TOO?

BRATTABRATTA

WHY DOESN'T EVERYONE STEP BACK AND TAKE A CLOSER LOOK AT THIS WHOLE *CONSPIRACY* I'VE BEEN PERPETRATING ON THE WORLD?

LET'S REALLY PEEL APART THIS *BIG* SECRET I KEPT FROM EVERYONE, *hmm?*

GAHH

SKRAK

FRAK

UNFF

I WAS RAISED IN KANSAS BY FARMERS, WENT TO SCHOOL, DELIVERED NEWSPAPERS, WENT TO CHURCH, MOVED TO METROPOLIS...

KRRUNKK

...WHERE I PUT ON A PAIR OF GLASSES, COMBED MY HAIR DIFFERENTLY AND WENT TO WORK FOR A DAILY NEWSPAPER, ALL THE WHILE WAITING FOR THE RIGHT MOMENT I COULD PUT MY POWERS TO USE.

KRRKAK

WELL, THAT MOMENT FINALLY CAME. AND I WORE THE RED AND BLUE SUIT TO HELP PEOPLE IN NEED, BUT ALSO NEVER STOPPED BEING CLARK KENT BECAUSE I WANTED TO LEAD A FULL LIFE WHILE ALSO PROTECTING THE PEOPLE I CARED ABOUT FROM BECOMING TARGETS.

DO YOU WEAR YOUR UNIFORM TO BED, TREVOR?

KEEP YOUR HOLSTER ON IN THE SHOWER?

DO YOU CLOSE YOUR EYES AND ACTUALLY FALL ASLEEP EVERY NIGHT?

NO.

NO.

YES.

WELL, I DON'T.

I CLOSE THEM, BUT I CAN HEAR *EVERYTHING*.

SO AFTER PARADEMONS, DOOMSDAY, ATLANTIS ATTACKING OUR SHORES, THE CRIME SYNDICATE, THE AMAZO VIRUS, ULYSSES, BRAINIAC, METALLO AND COUNTLESS OTHER BATTLES...

...YOU'RE TELLING ME, MISTER PRESIDENT, THAT I'M *NOT* BEING GIVEN THE BENEFIT OF THE DOUBT.

DO YOU THINK I'D BE STANDING HERE WITH YOU--GOING AGAINST THE ADVICE OF MY ENTIRE CABINET--IF I WASN'T *GIVING* YOU THE BENEFIT OF THE DOUBT, SUPERMAN?

WE HAVE A SCARED AND CONFUSED PUBLIC WHO DON'T LIKE IT WHEN THEIR SUPERHEROES SUDDENLY *AREN'T* WHO THEY SAY THEY ARE.

NO *HARM* WILL COME TO ANY OF YOUR FRIENDS.

THEY WILL BE RELEASED ONCE WE'VE BEEN ABLE TO GET SOME QUESTIONS ANSWERED.

SOONER RATHER THAN LATER.

ON THAT YOU HAVE MY WORD, SUPERMAN. LET'S HEAD BACK.

THERE ARE SEVERAL QUOTES STITCHED INTO THE OVAL OFFICE RUG YOU MAY HAVE SEEN, AND THE ONE I'VE ALWAYS TAKEN TO HEART BELONGS TO REVEREND MARTIN LUTHER KING: "THE ARC OF THE MORAL UNIVERSE IS LONG, BUT IT BENDS TOWARDS JUSTICE."

THAT'S A NOBLE THOUGHT TO EMBRACE, MISTER PRESIDENT, AND ONE I WISH--

PARASITE!

HUUUNNNGRRRY!

WHERE'S CLARK? DID HE SEND YOU--IS HE OKAY?

HE'S HELPING TO SECURE YOUR RELEASE...

...AS I'M DOING IN MY OWN WAY.

FEED!

GET DOWN, MISTER PRESIDENT! DON'T LET HIM TOUCH YOU!

WHAT DO YOU MEAN YOUR OWN WAY, YOUNG LADY?

THEY NEED TO GET TO THE TRUTH.

WHOSE TRUTH?

ALL OF YOURS.

...THAT'S RIGHT, I WAS THE FIRST ONE HE TOLD, AND I WAS DAMN PROUD THAT SUPERMAN FELT HE COULD TRUST *ME* WITH SUCH AN IMPORTANT SECRET.

I WOULD'VE TAKEN A BULLET FOR HIM TO KEEP IT.

YOU ARE!

WHAMM

HOW DID YOU FEEL, MISTER WHITE, WHEN HIS IDENTITY WAS REVEALED?

HOW DO YOU *THINK* I FELT, IDIOT?

I FELT LIKE A *FOOL.*

MY WHOLE LIFE'S BEEN DEDICATED TO PRESENTING *THE TRUTH* TO THE PUBLIC-- STRIVING FOR IT, UNCOVERING IT FROM THE DARKEST PLACES--AND THERE I WAS, FRONT AND CENTER USING MY OWN DAMN PAPER TO SELL THE LIE--*BETRAYED* BY SOMEONE I THOUGHT OF AS A FRIEND.

SKRAKAKK

SAHHR

AND DO YOU THINK YOUR *FRIEND* SUPERMAN WAS HONEST WITH YOU AT ALL TIMES, MISTER OLSEN? ALWAYS ABOVE BOARD?

...WELL SURE... I BEAT HIM A LOT IN CHESS AND PLENTY OF VIDEO GAMES BEFORE...

...OR DID HE *LET* ME WIN?

RRRR

AND YOU SUSPECTED NOTHING ALL THOSE YEARS IN SMALLVILLE, MISTER SANTIAGO?

YOUR QUESTIONS ABOUT A DECENT MAN MAKE ME INCREDIBLY SAD AND TIRED.

WONDER AND MAGIC ALL AROUND US AND ALL YOU PEOPLE WANT TO DO IS TEAR IT APART.

THE TRUTH-- EVERYONE SAYS THEY WANT IT, BUT NO ONE *REALLY* WANTS TO HEAR IT.

KOOOM

WHY DID YOU HIDE HIS IDENTITY FOR SO LONG, MISS LANG?

BECAUSE I KNEW A BOY WITH A BIG HEART LIKE CLARK NEEDED PROTECTING SO HE COULD ONE DAY PROTECT ALL OF US.

GROWING UP TOGETHER... THERE'S A *SPECIAL BOND*... NO SECRETS BETWEEN US... I'VE SEEN CLARK AT HIS LOWEST *AND* HIS HIGHEST.

FRAAAAP

SO HE'S NEVER LET YOU DOWN?

...HE SHOULD...

...HE SHOULD HAVE SAVED MY PARENTS.

WHAT WAS HE LIKE IN SCHOOL, MRS. TAKAHARA?

CLARK WAS AN ABOVE-AVERAGE STUDENT, WHO NEVER SEEMED TO BE TRULY PRESENT IN CLASS. IT ALWAYS LOOKED AS IF HE WAS LISTENING TO SOMEONE ELSE BESIDES ME, AND NOW THAT HIS SECRET IDENTITY IS OUT, I KNOW THE TRUTH.

HIS EARS WERE CONSTANTLY ATTUNED TO THE HEART OF SMALLVILLE, FOR SOMEONE IN NEED.

AND AT LEAST HIS ASKING TO GO TO THE BATHROOM ALL THE TIME FINALLY MAKES SENSE.

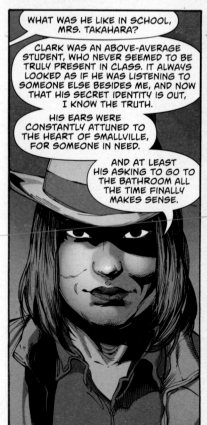

GRARR

WHAMM

DO YOU TRUST HIM, MISTER IRONS?

A GREAT DEAL MORE THAN I TRUST ANYONE WHO BREAKS INTO THE HOME OF MY GIRLFRIEND'S PARENTS AND SLAPS A TASER DISC ON MY HEAD AND KIDNAPS US.

OBVIOUSLY KEEPING A SECRET IDENTITY **SECRET** IS THE WAY TO GO.

SKRRAM

SPRRASHH

DID YOU EVER SUSPECT MISTER KENT WAS LEADING A DOUBLE LIFE, MISS GRANT?

NO, I DIDN'T, BUT I DID **SUSPECT** MISTER KENT WAS HIDING THE FACT THAT HE WAS ATTRACTED TO ME.

AND CALL ME CRAZY, BUT I **ALWAYS** THOUGHT CLARK HAD IT OVER SUPERMAN.

SKKASS KASSH

SUPERMAN, ARE YOU--

STAY BACK, MISTER PRESIDENT.

...SHOULD HAVE...ABSORBED MORE...GOTTEN BIGGER...STRONGER... WHAT HAPPENED TO YOUR--

--POWERAARGHH

WHAT THE HELL IS GOING ON HERE, TREVOR?!

I DIDN'T AUTHORIZE THIS ACTIVATION OR ATTACK!

I APOLOGIZE, SIR, COLONEL TREVOR HAD NO IDEA-- IT WAS SOLELY MY RESPONSIBILITY.

WITHOUT KNOWING SUPERMAN'S INTENTIONS, I HAD THE TACTICAL TEAM ESCORT PARASITE FROM TASK FORCE X IN CASE A SITUATION... *DEVELOPED.*

WHAT I *EXPECT,* ANGELO, IS MY *CHIEF OF STAFF* TO FOLLOW PROTOCOL AND NOT INSTIGATE A DAMN BATTLE ON THE SOUTH LAWN!

SUPERMAN, MY SINCERE APOLOGIES, THIS WAS--

I'VE HEARD ENOUGH, SIR.

I EXPECT YOU TO KEEP YOUR WORD REGARDING MY FRIENDS.

DONE.

COLONEL TREVOR.

LATITUDE 38.76N, LONGITUDE 77.48W.

WE ASSUME YOU'LL CONTINUE TO BE ON THE SIDE OF THE ANGELS.

ONLY SIDE I'VE EVER BEEN ON, MISTER PRESIDENT.

"ARE YOU READY TO BEGIN, MISS LANE?"

DARK TRUTH PART FOUR

PETER J. TOMASI writer DOUG MAHNKE penciller JAIME MENDOZA MARK IRWIN SEAN PARSONS SCOTT HANNA inkers WIL QUINTANA ULISES ARREOLA TOMEU MOREY colorists
ROB LEIGH letterer cover by DOUG MAHNKE AARON KUDER KLAUS JANSON & DEAN WHITE

WONDERFUL.

BZZZT
BZZZT

RICHARD, PLEASE INFORM THE PRESIDENT'S SECRETARY THAT I'M RUNNING A FEW MINUTES BEHIND SCHEDULE.

YOU GOT IT, MR. BEND.

LEVEL "A" POWER SOURCE AT FOLLOWING UPLOADED COORDINATES.

SEIZURE PROTOCOL APPROVED.

INGEST.

...ALL I'M SAYING IS WE *BETTER* BE THERE ON TIME, RONNIE.

I ATE A TON OF MAC AND CHEESE TO SAVE ENOUGH FOR THESE TICKETS.

THIS SHOW'S BEEN SOLD OUT FOR SIX MONTHS AND MY NEW GIRLFRIEND HASN'T STOPPED TALKING ABOUT IT.

STOP WORRYING YOUR PRETTY LITTLE HEAD ABOUT IT.

I *ALWAYS* KEEP MY WORD.

YEAH, EXCEPT WHEN YOU *DON'T*.

HANG ON!

WHAT ARE YOU DOING?!

FISHING BOAT TROUBLE-- PEOPLE IN THE WATER.

GOT A NO-BRAINER HERE, SO SIT BACK AND ENJOY THE SHOW, JASON.

--SEAS ARE CALM--WEATHER'S ALMOST PERFECT--

CHECK IT OUT-- H_2O INTO HELIUM--FLOAT THE BOAT AND ZIP THE FISH FOLKS RIGHT BACK INTO IT.

SOMETHING'S NOT RIGHT, RONNIE--GETTING SOME ENERGY FEEDBACK--A DISTORTION OF THE MATRIX...

Ah, YOU'RE JUST TIRED OF RIDING SHOTGUN.

WHAT I'M TIRED OF IS YOU NEVER LISTENING TO--

--SUDDENLY CAN'T FOCUS--DIZZY--

ARRGH

--JASON--TALK TO ME--

--WHAT THE HELL ARE--

--THESE THINGS!

GAHHHRRRR

DON'T YOU AGREE, THAT BASED ON THE AMOUNT OF ARTICLES YOU WROTE FOCUSED ON SUPERMAN'S ACTIVITIES, THAT YOUR SINGLE-MINDEDNESS COULD BE INTERPRETED AS AN OBSESSION, MISS LANE?

SUPERMAN HAS BEEN--AND ALWAYS WILL BE THE *LEAD STORY* WHEN HE'S IN ACTION. WHEREVER HE IS AND WHATEVER HE'S DOING IS THE *BIGGEST* NEWS STORY OF THAT PARTICULAR DAY. PERIOD.

IF YOU LOOK A LITTLE CLOSER ON YOUR BOARD YOU MAY SEE UNDER "OCCUPATION" THAT I'M A REPORTER.

I REPORT THE NEWS, IDIOT.

AT ANY TIME DID YOU KNOW THAT CLARK KENT AND SUPERMAN WERE ONE AND THE SAME BEFORE YOUR RECENT ARTICLE?

I DID NOT.

SURELY YOU UNDERSTOOD THE REVERBERATIONS YOUR ARTICLE WOULD HAVE. WHY SUBMIT IT FOR PUBLICATION?

AGAIN, SEE DEFINITION OF "REPORTER," MORON.

C'MON, CUT TO THE CHASE AND ASK WHAT'S REALLY ON ALL YOUR PEA-BRAINED MINDS.

DID YOU AND CLARK KENT EVER HAVE A ROMANTIC RELATIONSHIP?

THESE QUESTIONS ARE BECOMING--

WE DID NOT.

PLEASE SIT DOWN, MISS LANE.

I PREFER TO TELL THE TRUTH STANDING UP AND LOOKING YOU IN THE EYE.

IF I NEED TO, RESTRAINTS WILL BE--HEY--WHAT ARE--

DO ME A FAVOR--

--AND SHUT THE HELL UP ALREADY!

UNFF

ANY MORE QUESTIONS? BECAUSE I'D LIKE TO TAKE THIS DAMN *ROPE* OFF.

NO, WE'RE DONE HERE.

ARE YOU SATISFIED--DOES IT MAKE IT CLEAR THAT THESE PEOPLE BEAR NO ILL WILL FOR THIS COUNTRY--THAT THERE'S NO PLAN TO OVERTHROW THE GOVERNMENT?

THEY'RE JUST *INNOCENT* PEOPLE CAUGHT BETWEEN A SECRET AND SOMEONE THEY CARE ABOUT, SO CALL WHOEVER YOU NEED TO CALL BUT THEY'RE LEAVING WITH ME IMME--

BRROO BRROO BRROO

INCURSION LEVEL THREE!

GET GOING.

SHOW ME WHERE THE OTHERS ARE BEING HELD.

Y-YES, S-SIR, SUPERMAN, SIR.

SEEMS THEY *GOT* THE PRESIDENT'S MEMO.

YES IT D-DOES. THIS WAY, M-MAKE YOUR NEXT RIGHT.

WHY?

WHY WHAT?

MAKE ME UNDERSTAND *WHY* YOU DIDN'T TELL ME YOU WERE HEADING HERE?

TREVOR SAID THE FASTEST WAY TO GET YOUR PEOPLE HOME WAS FOR ME TO BREAK IN AND GET THEM TALKING IN FRONT OF THE CCTV'S...

...CONVINCE THE GOVERNMENT THEY WEREN'T PART OF SOME SECRET SCHEME AND ACTING AS FOOT SOLDIERS IN YOUR SHADOW, WORKING TO DESTABILIZE THE COUNTRY IN SOME WAY.

AND OF COURSE THE ONLY THING THAT TREVOR SAID WOULD BE DEFINITIVE WAS THE USE OF *YOUR LASSO.*

YES.

SO YOU DIDN'T THINK I COULD PERSUADE THE PRESIDENT TO RELEASE THEM.

KREEESH

I DIDN'T KNOW WHAT TO EXPECT, AND I DIDN'T WANT TO RISK NOT FREEING THEM WHEN I HAD THE CHANCE.

I WANTED TO HELP, CLARK.

BY DOING AN END RUN AROUND ME BECAUSE YOU KNEW I WOULDN'T CONDONE THE *LASSO METHOD.*

I ASKED EACH OF THEM FOR PERMISSION.

AND YOU THINK *THAT* MAKES IT OKAY, DIANA?

TO GET ALONG THEY FIGURED THEY NEEDED TO GO ALONG.

THEY WERE UNDER DURESS. *THEY WANTED OUT.*

I KNEW THERE'D BE NOTHING INCRIMINATING OR INCENDIARY ABOUT THEIR ANSWERS.

AND IF SOMEONE IN SOME GOVERNMENT CUBICLE WATCHING THE INTERVIEW UPLOADS DON'T AGREE WITH YOUR ASSESSMENT, WHAT THEN?

WE FIND A WAY TO RESOLVE THE SITUATION... *TOGETHER.*

I *ASKED* YOU TO LAY LOW-- KEEP SOME DISTANCE BECAUSE I DIDN'T WANT YOU GETTING TAINTED BY THIS. I NEEDED TO DEAL WITH IT *ALONE.*

YOU USED YOUR LASSO ON *ALL* OF THEM ALREADY?

IF A RED FLAG WENT UP ON ANY OF YOUR FRIENDS, WE'D BE DEALING WITH IT RIGHT NOW.

YES.

I DID.

EVERYONE'S GOING HOME!

KLANGG

SUPERMAN!

CLARK-- ARE YOU ALL RIGHT?

ME? I'M FINE, IT'S *YOU* GUYS I WAS WORRIED ABOUT.

HEY, *CLIPBOARD DUDE*-- SINCE YOU *SLAPPED* THIS ON ME IT'S ONLY FAIR--

PLIK

--*YOU* NOW GET TO *CHEW* ON IT FOR A WHILE.

SAVED BY MY BIG, STRONG **SECRETIVE** HERO!

Um, THANKS, CAT, BUT WE NEED TO GET MOVING.

WITH RESPECT, CLARK, I DO HOPE YOUR LOAD GETS LIGHTER...

...NOW THAT YOU DON'T HAVE TO BEAR A SECRET IDENTITY.

I'M SORRY YOU ALL GOT MIXED UP IN THIS BECAUSE OF ME, MRS. TAKAHARA.

DON'T WORRY ABOUT THIS NONSENSE.

KEEP DOING WHAT YOU'RE DOING, YOUNG MAN.

SUPES.

JOHN.

FIGURED YOU'D GET HERE SOONER OR LATER.

WISH IT WAS **SOONER.**

...ATOMIC SKULL... MAJOR DISASTER... CLARK AND I PUT THEM AWAY MONTHS AGO.

WHY ARE THEY UP THERE?

WHAT'S GOING ON, JOHN...

...AND WHAT IS THIS PLACE?

IT'S A REHABILITATION RESEARCH CENTER THAT WAS BUILT OFF THE GRID FOR SUPER-POWERED CRIMINALS.

YOU MEAN? A PRISON?

WELL, YEAH, SORT OF.

BUT THAT RADIANT HALO AROUND THE PODS...

LOOK, I HATE TO BREAK UP THE HUG FEST, BUT DON'T YOU THINK WE'VE SPENT ENOUGH TIME BEING HELD HERE AGAINST OUR WILL?!

I DON'T WANT TO HEAR IT, JUST GET US OUTTA HERE ALREADY.

PERRY, I WANT TO--

SKRAKK

--I'M NOT GOING ANYWHERE!

WHERE'S CLARK-- IS HE STILL BACK THERE?!

HE SAID TO HELP YOU GET EVERYONE CLEAR!

WAMM

KRAKK

UGNN

KOOOM

AND YOU LISTENED TO HIM?!

OF COURSE I DID-- HE'S FREAKIN' SUPERMAN!

SKREEEEE

GRAARGHH

BRING THEM OUT, STEEL!

WONDER WOMAN-- WAIT--

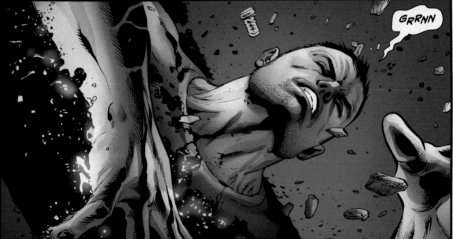

GRRNN

HANG ON-- I'VE GOT YOU!

RRNN

LET ME GO, DIANA--I DON'T WANT THIS THING TAKING BOTH OF US!

NOT HAPPENING, SO SHUT UP!

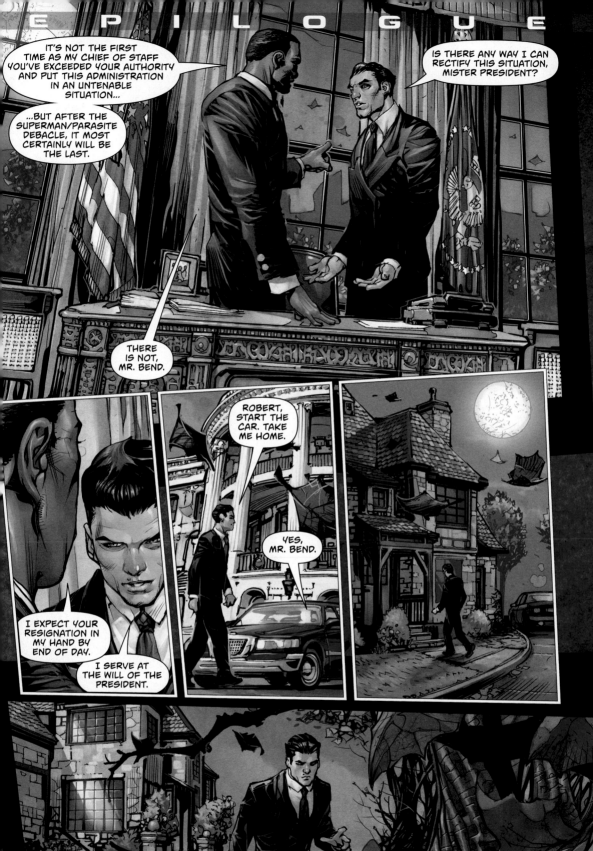

IT'S NOT THE FIRST TIME AS MY CHIEF OF STAFF YOU'VE EXCEEDED YOUR AUTHORITY AND PUT THIS ADMINISTRATION IN AN UNTENABLE SITUATION...

...BUT AFTER THE SUPERMAN/PARASITE DEBACLE, IT MOST CERTAINLY WILL BE THE LAST.

IS THERE ANY WAY I CAN RECTIFY THIS SITUATION, MISTER PRESIDENT?

THERE IS NOT, MR. BEND.

I EXPECT YOUR RESIGNATION IN MY HAND BY END OF DAY.

I SERVE AT THE WILL OF THE PRESIDENT.

ROBERT, START THE CAR. TAKE ME HOME.

YES, MR. BEND.

SEEMS I'M NOT THE FIRST TO ARRIVE.

HEART OF THE SUN

PETER J. TOMASI writer **DOUG MAHNKE** penciller **JAIME MENDOZA** **SEAN PARSONS** **JOHNNY DESJARDINS** inkers **WIL QUINTANA** colorist
ROB LEIGH letterer cover by **CARY NORD**

FOR THIRTY SECONDS I CAN'T HEAR ANYTHING.

THIRTY SECONDS OF EVERYONE SEEMINGLY SAFE AND SOUND AROUND THE WORLD.

A PEACE AND QUIET I'VE FOUGHT HARD FOR...

...BUT I KNOW 'S AN ILLUSION...

...A FLEETING MOMENT O SERENITY THAT ONLY LAS AS LONG AS IT TAKES FO MY ATOMS TO BE BROKE APART AND REARRANGE BY THIS TRANSPORTER.

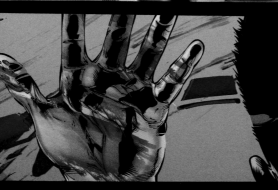

THEN THE BLOOD ON MY HANDS MAKES THE LAST FEW WEEKS COME RUSHING BACK...

.MY SECRET IDENTITY BLOWN, MY POWERS MEHOW BEING DRAINED, RUST BROKEN BETWEEN NA AND ME, MY FRIENDS PUT IN HARM'S WAY-- RISKING THEIR LIVES TO SAVE MINE

...EVERYTHING'S UPS DOWN, BUT THAT EN

LASER CANNONS CHARGING AND PREPARED TO FIRE UNLESS VOICE--

CLARK KENT.

KAL-EL.

VOICE MATCH AUTHENTICATED.

JUSTICE LEAGUE MEMBER RECOGNIZED.

WELCOME, SUPERMAN.

YEAH, HEY... RIGHT BACK ATCHA.

DIDN'T KNOW YOU WERE MAKING A TRIP UP TO THE HQ.

I'M ON MONITOR DUTY-- SAW YOU'RE HAVING SOME TELEPORTER CLEARANCE ISSUES.

I NEED... ONE OF THE SHUTTLES, FLASH

OMIGOD, WHAT THE HELL HAPPENED, CLARK?!

SALVATION TECH EMERGENCY EVALUATION LABORATORIES.
MANASSAS, VIRGINIA.

WHUPWHURWHUP

BOTH OF YOU SHOULD BE ON THAT HELICOPTER.

I AGREE WITH WONDER WOMAN.

IT'S A **MIRACLE** ALL OF US ARE WALKING UPRIGHT AND NOT IN BODY BAGS AFTER WHAT WENT DOWN.

WE'RE GOING AFTER HIM, MISTER IRONS. CLARK NEEDS OUR HELP.

ACTUALLY, HE SAID HE DIDN'T WANT **ANY** OF US NEAR HIM RIGHT NOW.

ACTUALLY, CLARK WAS TALKING TO WONDER WOMAN-- AND **HER**.

NOT ME, JOHN.

DO YOU NEED ANY FURTHER ASSISTANCE CLEANING UP THIS FACILITY, STEEL?

YOU'VE DONE ENOUGH HEAVY LIFTING.

THANKS FOR HELPING ME GET THE CRIMINALS' STASIS PODS BACK ONLINE, WONDER WOMAN.

YOU'RE WELCOME.

ARE YOU SURE YOU CAN'T COME WITH US?

THE SECURITY SYSTEM AND POWER GRID IS STILL UNSTABLE, LANA.

I NEED TO BE HERE OR THESE SUPER-POWERED BADASSES ARE GOING TO BUST OUT AND UNLEASH A WORLD OF HURT, AND NO WAY I'M LETTING THAT HAPPEN.

FEEL FREE TO STAY WITH YOUR BOYFRIEND, MISS LANG.

COMPUTER, THIS IS SUPERMAN, PREPARE TO ENGAGE HYPER-LIGHT DRIVE ON UPLOADED COORDINATES.

PLOTTING COURSE.

PLEASE WAIT.

CLARK-- IT'S DIANA-- WHAT ARE YOU DOING?!?

I NEED TO... GET AS CLOSE AS I CAN, DIANA...

...POWER UP... AS MUCH AS I CAN...

LET'S TALK ABOUT THIS AFTER

WE TAKE CARE

OF YOUR BACK WOUND.

--nnGg-- I'VE SAID EVERYTHING I WANTED TO SAY--

--nNgg-- AT STEEL'S PLACE, DIANA --nNGg

ALMOST DONE HERE, STAND STILL.

AND WHAT YOU SAID TO ME IN THE HYPER-LIGHT--DID YOU MEAN IT?

I'M SORRY, BUT YEAH...

I DID.

I DO.

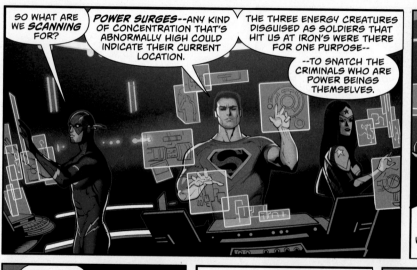

SO WHAT ARE WE *SCANNING* FOR?

POWER SURGES--ANY KIND OF CONCENTRATION THAT'S ABNORMALLY HIGH COULD INDICATE THEIR CURRENT LOCATION.

THE THREE ENERGY CREATURES DISGUISED AS SOLDIERS THAT HIT US AT IRON'S WERE THERE FOR ONE PURPOSE--

--TO SNATCH THE CRIMINALS WHO ARE POWER BEINGS THEMSELVES.

THEY TRIED *SNATCHING* CLARK, TOO.

THESE THINGS EITHER NEED TO FEED ON ENERGY OR THEY WANT THE POWER FOR SOMETHING ELSE.

ANYTHING?

NOTHING'S CHARTING, JUST THE MARKER LEVELS OF KNOWN SOURCES.

THEY COULD HAVE A CLOAKING DEVICE OR BE DOING SOMETHING TO DAMPEN THE POWER LEVELS SO THEY'RE NOT EASILY READABLE BY AN OUTSIDE SOURCE.

MAYBE THEY'RE EVEN DEEP UNDERGROUND.

THERE COULD BE ANOTHER WAY TO GO ABOUT THIS.

THERE'S A KNOWN FILE POWER SOURCE I JUST KNOCKED HEADS WITH AND...

I'VE GOT HIM ZEROED IN, WHICH MEANS I'M GOING TO NEED THOSE SPECIAL GLOVES WE'VE BEEN WORKING ON.

YOU *DO* KNOW I'M COMING WITH YOU.

WE JUST WENT THROUGH THIS AND I'M--

NO MATTER WHAT'S GOING ON BETWEEN US AT THE MOMENT, WE ARE LEAGUE TEAMMATES *FIRST* AND *FOREMOST* AND ALWAYS WILL BE.

WANT ME TO HIT THE BEACON, BRING THE CAVALRY IN ON THIS OP?

NO WORRIES, FLASH...

UNDERSTOOD?!

...I'VE GOT THE GOD OF WAR BY MY SIDE.

THIS IS BR1 REQUESTING CLEARANCE APPROACH.

AFFIRMATIVE, BR1. YOU ARE A GO.

YAHH

SMASSH

SORRY FOR THE UNANNOUNCED VISIT--

--BUT YOUR CHAT-LINE TO BELLE REVE IS GOING SILENT FOR A WHILE UNTIL I GET WHAT I CAME FOR.

RRRGHFF

LONG TIME NO SEE, PARASITE.

RRRGFF

YEAH, I MISSED YOU TOO.

WHERE ARE YOU TAKING HIM?

WE'RE GOING FOR A RIDE...

...WE'LL TRY NOT TO BREAK HIM!

GAARRR

KOOOM

GRRAAAH

YOU THINK SOME SPECIAL MITTENS ARE GOING TO KEEP ME FROM SUCKING YOU BOTH DRY?!?

SKRRK

YOU'LL BE BEGGING ME FOR DEATH-- PLEADING WITH ME TO END YOUR LIVES!

COULD YOU PLEASE SHUT UP FOR A MOMENT?

FRAKK

RAVENOUS
PETER J. TOMASI writer DOUG MAHNKE penciller JAIME MENDOZA MARK IRWIN KEITH CHAMPAGNE DOUG MAHNKE inkers WIL QUINTANA colorist
TRAVIS LANHAM letterer cover by ED BENES & PETE PANTAZIS

WHAT KIND OF *DEAL* ARE YOU TALKING ABOUT?!?

THE *KIND* OF DEAL THAT HELPS US *BOTH*.

AND JUST HOW ARE YOU GONNA HELP ME, HUH?

BY KICKING MY ASS AROUND SOME MORE AND THROWING ME IN A CELL?

UNGH.

WOULD WE HAVE BROKEN YOU OUT OF THE CHOPPER IF WE WERE JUST GOING TO LOCK YOU UP AGAIN?

HRRM...

YOU MAY NOT BE AS *TASTY* AS BEFORE--BUT YOUR GIRLFRIEND-- SHE'S GOT A WHOLE OTHER TYPE OF LIFE-FORCE ENERGY THAT'S OFF THE--

MANNERS.

KRAKK

YOU STILL HAVEN'T EXPLAINED HOW YOU'RE GONNA HELP ME?!?

BY GIVING YOU WHAT YOU WANT AND LOTS OF IT.

SO WHAT DO I GOT TO DO?

WHAT YOU DO NATURALLY-- TRACK ENERGY AND EAT IT.

AND WHAT'S STOPPING YOU BIG BAD JUSTICE LEAGUERS FROM TRACKING IT?

IT'S CLOAKED-- HIDDEN SOMEWHERE THAT WE CAN'T LOCK IN ON.

DESPERATE TIMES, DESPERATE MEASURES.

YOU'RE GOING TO BE OUR GLORIFIED BLOODHOUND ON A VERY SHORT LEASH, PARASITE.

AND IF I DON'T, THEN WHAT?

SO YOU'RE USING ME.

THEN I HEAR SCREAMING IN YOUR FUTURE.

TELL ME AGAIN ABOUT THIS ENERGY SOURCE.

IT'S BIG AND IT'S DANGEROUS.

AND YOU'RE BOTH JUST GONNA STAND BY AND LET ME CONSUME IT ONCE I FIND IT?

TO A POINT, YES.

AND THEN YOU'RE JUST GONNA LET ME STROLL OFF INTO THE SUNSET, HMM?

I AM.

I WANT ASSURANCES.

AND I WANT TO HEAR WONDER CHICK'S PRETTY LIPS SAY IT--

MMMM

MMMM

--MY MEAL TICKET!
SKLOOM
THANKS FOR THE SAVE, PARASITE!
DON'T THANK ME. WE'RE ALL PART OF THE SAME TEAM.
FOR NOW.
PUT THESE POWERED CRIMINALS DOWN HARD AND FAST--
--AND SHOW NO MERCY FOR THESE LAB-CREATED--
--BLACK HOLE CREATURES!

I *DIDN'T* NEED YOUR ASSISTANCE, PARASITE!

CHOMPP!

AND I *DIDN'T* REALLY WANNA GIVE IT, BUT HERE WE ARE!

WHAT THE HELL...?

BLUP

BLUP

COME ON! LET'S FINISH THEM OFF--

--SHUT THIS FREAK DOWN--

--AND GET FIRESTORM OUT OF--

DIANA!

NO.

POWER HUNGRY

PETER J. TOMASI writer   ARDIAN SYAF   TOM DERENICK pencillers   TOM DERENICK   JAIME MENDOZA   JORDI TARRAGONA   MARK IRWIN inkers   WIL QUINTANA colorist   TOM NAPOLITANO letterer   cover by YANICK PAQUETTE & NATHAN FAIRBAIRN

...DIANA...

...CAN YOU HEAR ME?

...BARELY...

...TAKING...ALL MY STRENGTH...

...NOT TO LET THE SUIT...

...CONTROL ME...

YOUR POWER LEVELS ARE OFF THE CHART, WONDER WOMAN.

I DIDN'T THINK I COULD CONTAIN AND DRAIN SOMEONE SO... GODLY.

BUT I GUESS NEVER SAY NEVER.

KEEP COMING AT ME, YOU BASTARDS, AND I'LL KEEP SUCKING THE LIFE OUTTA YA!

AllIEEE

ARRGH

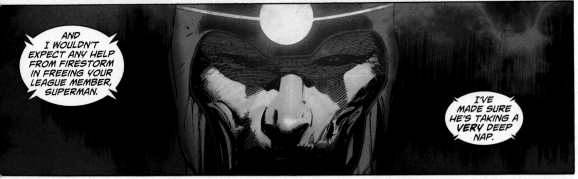

AND I WOULDN'T EXPECT ANY HELP FROM FIRESTORM IN FREEING YOUR LEAGUE MEMBER, SUPERMAN.

I'VE MADE SURE HE'S TAKING A VERY DEEP NAP.

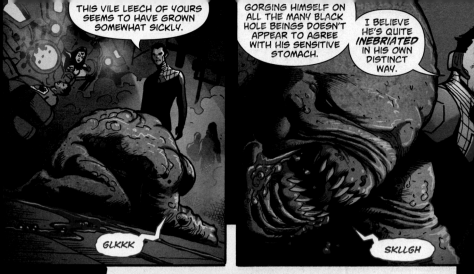

THIS VILE LEECH OF YOURS SEEMS TO HAVE GROWN SOMEWHAT SICKLY.

GORGING HIMSELF ON ALL THE MANY BLACK HOLE BEINGS DOESN'T APPEAR TO AGREE WITH HIS SENSITIVE STOMACH.

I BELIEVE HE'S QUITE *INEBRIATED* IN HIS OWN DISTINCT WAY.

GLKKK

SKLLGH

AND THE BRIGHT STAR THAT IS OUR YOUNG FRIEND FIRESTORM.

DISTINCT ON A WHOLE OTHER LEVEL.

WHAT ARE YOU DOING TO HIM?

FIRESTORM WILL BE MY NUCLEAR TRIGGER, AND *TRANSMUTE* THE STORED ENERGY I'VE BEEN *SECRETLY* SIPHONING FROM MY FATHER'S SUPPLY...

...INTO MY EXACT DNA FORM SO I CAN ABSORB IT WITHIN FIFTEEN MINUTES...

klik

...AND I'LL FINALLY HAVE ALL THE POWERS I NEED TO COMBAT MY LOVING FATHER.

SPLARSH

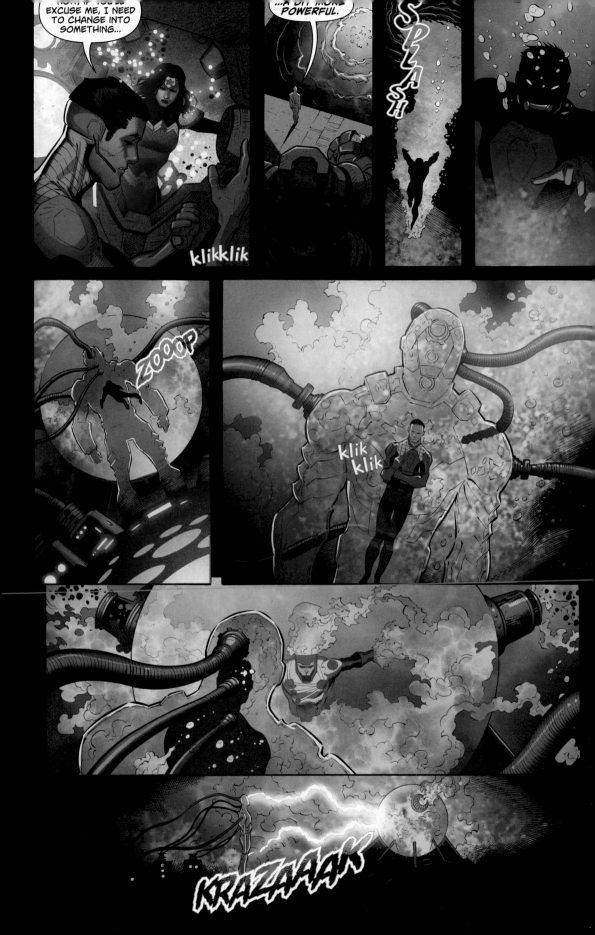

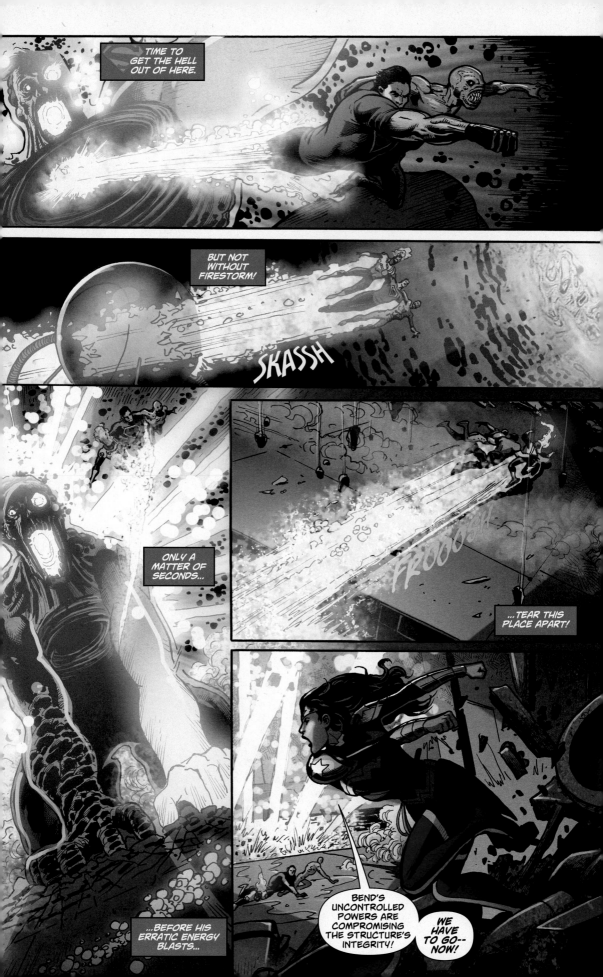

*"Maybe **I** should hold the rope..?"*

TRUTH PREVIEW
PETER J. TOMASI writer **PAULO SIQUEIRA** artist **HI-FI** colorist **ROB LEIGH** letterer

In the spring of 2015, this preview to the DARK TRUTH story arc was released as an online teaser. Ultimately, the scenes in the preview were retold in SUPERMAN/ WONDER WOMAN #22—with some scenes excised, and other parts of the story told with a different tone. Here you will find the confrontation between Superman and the Flash that ultimately took place "off camera" in the printed comic, and a different spin on the scene between Superman and Wonder Woman.

CLARK KENT.

JUSTICE LEAGUE MEMBER RECOGNIZED.

WELCOME, SUPERMAN.

HEY, DIDN'T KNOW YOU WERE MAKING A TRIP UP TO THE HQ.

I'M ON MONITOR DUTY-- SAW YOU'RE HAVIN' SOME TELEPORTE CLEARANCE ISSUES.

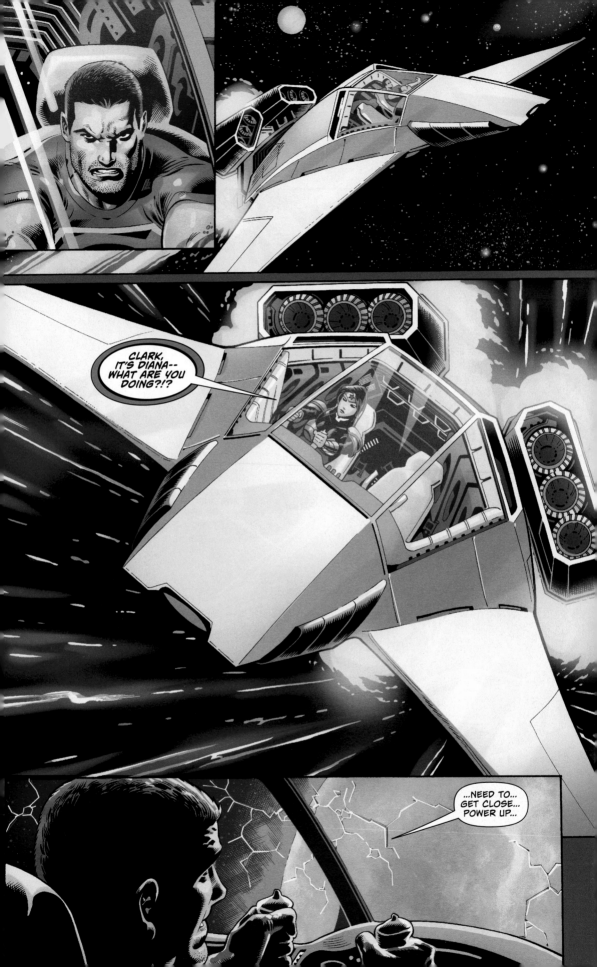

PENCILS FOR SUPERMAN/WONDER WOMAN #18, PAGE 14

PENCILS FOR SUPERMAN/WONDER WOMAN #19, PAGES 2-3

UNUSED LAYOUT FOR SUPERMAN/WONDER WOMAN #19, PAGE 6